Holocaust Survival Stories

The Authentic Holocaust Survival Story

(A Heartbreaking True Story of Courage and Survival)

Lawrence Johnson

Published By **Bella Frost**

Lawrence Johnson

All Rights Reserved

Holocaust Survival Stories: The Authentic Holocaust Survival Story (A Heartbreaking True Story of Courage and Survival)

ISBN   978-1-990373-86-2

Legal & Disclaimer

The information contained in this book is not designed to replace or take the place of any form of medicine or professional medical advice. The information in this book has been provided for educational & entertainment purposes only.

The information contained in this book has been compiled from sources deemed reliable, and it is accurate to the best of the Author's knowledge; however, the Author cannot guarantee its accuracy and validity and cannot be held liable for any errors or omissions. Changes are periodically made to this book. You must consult your doctor or get professional medical advice before using any of the suggested remedies, techniques, or information in this book.

Table Of Contents

Chapter 1: What does it serve?

"Because," suddenly the Rabbi joins in the discussion in the manner of waking, "it can always happen that he is you."

"What? !" we all three exclaim in amazement: Guys speaking in their native Hebrew and me shocked - in Russian.

"I will tell you a story," the Rabbi starts, and I think about touch my hands. This signifies that the lecture can be a bit late, even if it's the lesson will be five minutes behind, the fact is that there's a bus station just a few steps away.

"It was at the end of the sixties," according to the elderly man. "Television first appeared, initially, and it claimed to be entirely educational. People of faith haven't yet taken the time to realize within it the cause of their evil. We as students at the Yeshiva (religious Jews school), were enthralled by the very few people who owned"magic boxes "magic boxes" and enjoyed the endless blather that poured out from these boxes that appeared harmless to us. Then one day, a certain old Jew known as Kraus is on the sole Israeli channel and informs us his son has gone through an operation that is difficult and requires blood transfusion. The problem is that the son suffers from an extremely rare blood type that is not able to find donors in any way. Thus,

Kraus, appeals to anyone who could help Kraus to save his sole son!"

"Well obviously next day the entire yeshiva (both the men as well as the rabbis joined together to offer blood. Oh, and - oh! it was a miracle! One of our members is carrying the blood kind! We naturally, we felicitate him because this is a chance that has come to him and the chance to save the life of a person! The hospital is contacted and we discover that the procedure is scheduled to take place within one week, which is during the day two of Passover. On the following day, the patient is extremely dejected during classes. He claims that his father has utterly forbidden the donation of blood to his son, who is Kraus himself. The entire class is stunned. The religious Jew does not want to protect the life of an individual! Why is this? The classmate sighs - dad was not able to explain the situation to him. It's often hard to speak to someone that survived the Holocaust and are silent for the rest of their lives."

When I glance at my watch, it's a pleasure. The relaxed style of presentation is refreshing However, when the timing is not as good ... It's okay, I'll have to get up.

"Then the rabbi called an unnamed young man, and demanded that he describe to him the reason for what was happening to him and whether there was any chance of be able to influence the parent who was obstinate. The boy shook his head then, when he had thought about it about it, replied: "You know sir, there's an alternative. In the Passover Seder (celebration dinner) The father, who has consumed the standard glass of wine generally adds more. It's typically, it's not wine however, something more powerful ... (in in front of your eyes is the large bottle which is filled with homemade wine vodka. It is said to be at forty degrees similar to ordinary vodka, however certain craftsmen, according to them can make it to seventy degrees). Dad's face will become soft when you ask him to engage him in conversation," he finished."

"Next to exactly one week later, our Rabbi looks at the time watching his Seder at home. He eats the food in short amounts while he performs the whole ceremony at a rapid rate, and then he grabs a half-finished bottle of brandy kosher and heads for his father, who is the yeshiva's young student.

The proprietor of the home was friendly to him, he inquired about his health, and then offered him a seat at the table. However, as soon as the rabbi spoke regarding the unfortunate child of the tragic Kraus the bayonets popped in the face of the person he was talking to. But our rabbi will not stop. He takes out his brandy, pours it to him and his already drunk man. He then gives a three-minute "Lekhaim" (toast "for life" in Hebrew) to emphasize the incredibly important obligation to love the neighbor you've just discussed with so much enthusiasm. The man who is adamant drink, eats and does not speak. Then, after a while the rabbi interrupts the silence by pouring water and then gives the speech, focusing on the most important commandment. The silence is broken again. After the third and final monologue on love, and then the libation the Rabbi screams: "Well ..." his opponent is not holding back."

"Okay," he says, "I will tell you the story, but you already know. I'm from Lviv. Before World War II, I had the shoe store. There was even a home ... The most valuable thing I owned it was the son of my Gregory. He was an athlete! He danced! He was Acrobat! He had a flexible body. At the age of nine years old, he started to entertain the general public, initially to entertain himself, and after that, he would bring cash at home. Although I didn't really need the money. This money was mostly used to buy treats and sweets to Gregory himself. However, the amount of pride I felt for him. They say you earn more at the age of an adult. He earned it!

Then the Germans arrived and the hell started and all manner of restrictions including humiliation, yellow stars, and later the Ghetto. The ghetto is, as it is called, there was the general plight of people. But, at the same time, Gregory didn't let my family suffer from hunger. It started with the fact that Gregory began speaking before people living in ghettos and not to earn money, simply to cheer the residents up. Soon he was at the German Commandant's Office. It seemed like the last straw. He comes back with a healthy and wholesome body, being and accompanied by a cop as well as a large bag of potatoes. The truth is that the Germans were determined to see whether my son was worthy of and made an incredible impression, so they not only released them, but also started regular visits to concerts before different areas of their garrisons, in front of their officers, and in the presence of various guests with high status. Then they covered all of it through food. The food was almost empty, and also provided food to those with whom we were in the same place as well as threw food at the other residents. And the Germans ... They did not want their most-loved actor to suddenly weaken or sick from scurvy therefore they fed him.

Then, in a nutshell, hope came into the world. Everything would be perfect If it wasn't Kraus! Who was Kraus? He was one of the chiefs in the Judenrat! (Jewish-Nazi group within the ghettos) It was a devil more savage than every German. Also, he was a hateful person to me Gregory! As they walked together on the street Kraus yelled insults and rebuked at Gregory! If Gregory was speaking to Jews for the purpose of trying to bring them back to life, and keep their energy up the Jews had to conduct it secretly - not it was not done by the Germans and not from Kraus! When he was aware of the performance on the spot, the villain issued orders to stop the event! "I will achieve my aim!" he yelled. "You will be sent to a concentration camp!" It appears that Gregory was successful in his mission. The day was horribly painful that Gregory was sent to the office of the commandant. The next day, a raid conducted, and a number of adolescents were seized. For some reason, I believe it was Kraus himself was the one who hunted Gregory. When I walked into the office of the commandant and begged him to have my boy released! I repeatedly told his German official: "You yourself love his performances so much!" He laughed at my face "We'll manage!"

The whole day I walked around the Ghetto. I was unable to return to my home. At the night ... It was as I was imagining that some sort of sixth sense had pushed me into an unassuming, dusty, cobbled attic, which was not fit to live in, and where I was not since we moved into the neighborhood. "Tc ..." - I was trying to see some light in the darkness. That was my Gregory! He had escaped the Germans and now hid because even his fellow housemates could not have imagined that Gregory was in the area. What a joy I felt! Unfortunately my excitement was short-lived. On the next day, Kraus showed up with a firearm I can only imagine that Kraus was armed with a pistol - the

Germans allowed him to carry that included an officer as well as two soldiers! They walked up to the attic and began to beat my Gregory's hand and then took him to the street. My wife and me rushed to defend our child, and we wondered we didn't know what to do! We were shackled by soldiers as well as Kraus, who was the villain, declared "Take them away!" Then they took us to the headquarters of the commandant. From afar I could hear a gun fired behind me and I understood that Gregory is Gregory no more. Gregory...

We were shipped to Auschwitz My wife was sent immediately to the gas station, as well as me, in the labour camp. They didn't intend to put the Cyclone "B" on me - they figured that I would be fine without it. So why hurry? The result would remain exactly the same. The truth is, all came to this at least once I wished for the life of my wife. Particularly as I thought of Gregory ...

After that, we were driven on the road to Germany ... Rabbi, have you heard of"Death March" "Death March"? Do you think about the feeling of walking over the bodies of people that walked right in the front and then think about how someone else just was ahead of you and then imagine that a person coming back to follow you?

The moment Bergen-Belsen was liberated by the French The first step they took was to dispose of the dead bodies. One of the bodies was stirred up during the loading. I was one of them."

The person who told the story poured another brandy, took a sip and said: "In freedom, no person was watching me. My wife was dead. Gregory died. Zionist representatives suggested I travel to Palestine. Why would I not? This is where I changed my name and got married. My boys were born. When I turned on the TV screen, I saw Kraus. Only now he is Karsov! He, the one who murdered my son, is now asking his son Moshe and me to in saving his son? It won't happen! "

"Almost to the time of dawn the rabbi was there in the morning, calling on the tragic man to free Moshe into the hospital. What was his response? Perhaps he stated that a son shouldn't be accountable to his father's death, the son should not save someone and that we shouldn't behave like Kraus himself. Kraus is a creation of the most High so the human being's life is sacred. ..."

"It's curious," I considered. "The the narrator has knowledge of this particular meeting because of the words spoken by his Rabbi. While at the same time he recounts the story of a yeshiva student's father as if would have known it personally however, about the remarks of the rabbi He says "Probably." And anyway I'm wondering what time the meeting took place at? " Yet I've never been able to glance at my watch.

"... The short version is that he took our father Moshe the prized "let him be who you want! It's not my business in this." Then on Day 2 of Passover in the vicinity of the house of Moshe The car stopped at the place where the rabbi is seated and then leaves the home ... But, the rabbi is not Moshe the father, but Moshe, our father. Moshe himself! Wearing a Saturday jacket! With a striking look (or perception - I'm not certain) The man heads for the vehicle, and Moshe is right behind the car. He chose to stay the way!

The patients arrive at the hospital. Moshe is rushed to the hospital, preparing for a blood transfusion. Overall, the procedure went well, everything's perfect and Kraus Karsov, also known as Karsov and bursting with tears of happiness, as he kneeling in front of the his father who is Moshe. The cards will be unveiled!

"Scoundrel!" his father shouts. "Look at me! You are the dad of Gregory! The father is this poor child that you, as a geek, shot! I ..." I am choking in rage, Kraus throws in his fists Kraus.

"Listen to me," Kraus said, as the men were being taken away. "Listen to me, please!" When the silence ceased Kraus began to tell his tale:

"I wasn't just an ally of the Judenrat and the Judenrat, but also an organizer in the resistance underground. We organized deliveries in the ghettos of supplies and medicines, as well as weapons. We were planning for a revolution! Most importantly, we helped people get out of the ghetto into freedomand we searched for families who could conceal them. We also made connections with people who were partisans. What was the source of connection to us with the Ghetto? Children! The brave boys who made it from the ghetto without being noticed by Germans as well as the police. The smugglers were known as. There was a huge collection of smugglers. Do you know which one was the most successful of them all, who was my most favorite, and was my most important contacts? Your Gregory!

The man just did wonders. It appeared that he could traverse a wall through the thick brick wall. This was the way that Nazis kept us out of all the other people in the world. I adored him. In public, of course I needed to be kind to his every manner so that Germans wouldn't be able to discern that he was doing anything. In fact, a few times after a meeting to him I was able to stop his appearances and disperse the crowd. But, I lied that I didn't know about his other speeches. The whole thing was to concealing. However ... regardless how much I tried to conceal it...

The next day, the Germans were able to capture Gregory! Before he was detained, I managed to help him be able to escape the commandant's house. What the next step? We determined that he should remain in his attic after which ... everything was to be completed fast. I needed to be in to arrest his fugitive, only to have him imperceptibly leave the Ghetto. I was aware that perhaps with me, a German could be sent for the task.

It's true that the command itself gave it with "Walter" gun to me. Don't blame them! My wife was to come later. However, everything went wrong. Instead of just one German Three were taken with me in one go including an officer and two soldiers. When I had three people around me, it was difficult to handle the situation, so as we headed to your home I wondered what to do in order to escape the circumstances. Oh, the happiness! My wife and I helped me in the rush to protect Gregory! My soldier went along with you and officers ... I made it through with the officer by myself. Gregory and I were able to get from the ghetto. And on the following morning we drove out to the hamlet it had served for many years as a point of entry to our wanted criminals. It was just that my wife was too busy! The Germans took her in and then threw at her with rage and sent her to Auschwitz! It was a blessing that she made it through, and then after war we encountered. The camp doctors performed experiments with her, and they told her she would never be able to have children."

"Oh, here you are and fell for a lie!" Moshe's father, who was hushed of Moshe shouted. "Could not you be a father? What about your son to whom we have saved our life this morning"? "

"This is not my son," replied Karsov. "This is Gregory!"

It appears that the silence that followed when the rabbi concluded his story won't end, it will continue to rumble forever. Finally, I decide to glance at the timer. Of course the bus has long gone and the following one is not known when or when it'll be. Oh, and he's a jerk!

Potatoes story

Chapter 2: Riga Ghetto

In the past an acquaintance of mine shared with my father the amazing tale. The writer was born in Latvia and also speaks Latvian very well. After the war, it was his turn to drive from Riga to the coast on a train. On the other side of his car sat an old calm and dark Latvian. I don't know when the conversation started, but I do know which the elderly man related a story.

"Listen," said the elderly man. "I reside in the suburbs of Riga. In the days before conflict, there was a person who lived in my neighborhood. He was an extremely bad character. It is even possible that the man was dishonest and a raged man. The man was involved in speculative transactions regarding food products on the black markets. It is obvious that these individuals lack heart or honour. Many say speculation is just a way to enrich yourself.

What exactly is it based? The human experience, the crying of children, but most importantly, on our insatiableness.

He was working along with his spouse. Then ... and then the Germans were in control of Riga and began to force all Jews into a "ghetto" in order to murder some and to starve the rest. The whole "ghetto" was cordoned off and the cat couldn't get out. People who were fifty feet closer to the sentries were shot in the spot. Jews particularly children were killed in the thousands each day. Then my friend had an excellent plan - fill a wagon full of potatoes, then bribe on the German sentry, then go there to go into the "ghetto" and exchange potatoes to jewels. Many people believed that the Jews who were trapped within the "ghetto", had a majority of them gone. So he did. When he was leaving I met him in the street. Now can just take a take note of what he had to say.

"I will," he declared, "only change the potatoes for women, who have children."

"Why?" I asked.

"But because they are ready for anything for the sake of the children and I will earn three times more on this. I said nothing, but it cost me a lot too. Can you see it?"

The Latvian removed the disintegrated tube in his mouth. He pointed it at his teeth. The teeth were too small. "I didn't say anything however I pushed the tube using my teeth to the point that I broke the tube as well as the two teeth I have. The theory is that blood rushes towards the head. I don't know. The blood flowed not towards my head but rather to my hands, and to my fists. The blood became as heavy when they were filled with iron. If he didn't quit at once I may be dead in just one strike. It appears that he guessed that, as he leapt off my feet and smiled as if he was the face of a ferret ... However, this doesn't matter. After dark, he stuffed his truck with bags of potatoes. He then headed for Riga within Riga's "ghetto". He was stopped by the sentry, but you're aware that poor people can see one another in a blink. He offered a bribe the guard, and the guard told him: "You are a fool. Go on, but they've only empty stomachs. You'll return with your potato that is rotten. I'm willing to bet on your behalf."

The "ghetto" he drove into the large courtyard of a home. Children and women surrounded the wagon, stuffed with potatoes. The crowd sat silently as he took off the bag that he had just untied. One woman was standing holding a corpse in her arms, and pulled an old gold watch she was holding in her hands. "Crazy! The man yelled in shock. "Why would you require potatoes when he's already dead? Escape!" He himself told the story later, he did not understand what was that he had to go through it. He grinned and started to cut the ties off the bags before pouring the potato on the ground. "Hurry up! The woman shouted. Please give me your children. I'll take them away. They must stay still and remain quiet. Make sure to hurry!"

The mothers, in a hurry, started to trap the scared children in bags. Then the man firmly tied them. The truth is, mothers didn't have the time to touch the children. They knew they wouldn't ever see them ever again. The wagon was loaded filled with kids' toys and leaving a number of potato bags in the back and then left. The ladies kissed the filthy wheels of his vehicle, and he drove away in silence, not looking at them. The horses yelled in his direction in fear that one of them might cry and hurt all. The children were quiet.

The sentry spotted the man from afar and said: "Well, so what? I warned you that you were a fool. Get out and take your stinky potato until the lieutenant showed up." He drove by his sentry and cursed the final words spoken by these miserable Jews as well as their children who were adamant about being slain. The driver did not return to home, but instead drove through the back roads until he came to the woods around Tukums which is the place where our partisans resided. given their children and the partisans kept their children in a safe location. His wife was shocked when He told her that the Germans confiscated his potatoes and placed him under detention over two whole days. At the end of the war after which he divorced his wife and moved out of Riga.

The older Latvian did not speak. "Now I think," the man said and smiled for the first time "that it would be bad, if I had not restrained myself and killed him with my

fist."

Chapter 3: Humans as well as nonhumans

It was two days. The Nazis were carrying people on freight vehicles ... women and children! Older men! The whole group was to be part of the SS like they were not alive, but some form of thing! In the event that they're objects that are not alive, they don't need feeding. They could be put in the car until so overflowing that they are unable to be able to stand. There is no need to worry, in the event that someone doesn't survive and then dies during the journey. Simply toss them out! It was finally here! arrived for those who waited however, some dreamed the train wouldn't stop! Some simply wanted to die. The old Jacob observed his travelling partner with a lustful look. He departed in the middle of nowhere, never waiting to make a stopping point. Carriages were opened! The eyes of the people who closed them from the bright light. However, when they reopened their eyes, a lot of them are inclined to be blind. In blindness, they cannot be able to see the future proprietors ... Cynical, cold monsters that have claimed to be as supermen and Aryans.

The heartbreaking cry of a female children were snatched away from their parents and removed. With dogs barking, the children were told to take off their clothes. Old Jacob was stunned and could not take it in. The SS soldiers who were ferocious started digging into the old linen and separate everything: skirts went to skirts, dresses went to dress and shoes for the shoes.

"I have told Walter, Walter, that these Jews have a good idea of what shoes look like. Beautiful skin! We'll be using it for a while! Hey, you! Old man! Remove your shoes!" Jacob did not remove his shoes, and was irritated at the supposed superhumans that believed they were gods in the earth. "Do you have weak hearing? Are you deaf? I'm talking about shoes!"

"What for?" Jacob said.

"What do you mean why? This skin is needed the Reich! They will make a lot of useful things from it for the front!"

"No, they won't!" said Jacob. He was unable to take it anymore and began to talk about the issues that were bubbling in his head. "You are evil people and you take off people's clothes for the purpose of supplying murderers! Be aware that these shoes won't help the people you're putting them on! God knows she will stay here! signal! A symbolic symbol! A symbol of your cruelty and suffering of the Jewish population ... and you ..."

It was shot! Jacob fell dead. Walter was as if nothing could ever had happened to him, took his shoe from old man, and put his shoes on top of the others. However, old Jacob had a point! The shoes, in which his shoes were placed were left unaffected! Everyone around the world could see and understood who truly were people and also who were not human...

Deadly stripteases in Auschwitz

Franziska Mann

The woman who is in her final moments showed that it is necessary to take on the enemy until the end, even in the face of no possibility of the survival. It is at the very minimum this will be an effort to win a worthy end. It's what young Jewish ballerina who grew up in Poland and was later taken to the Auschwitz concentration camp in order to die inside a gas chamber performed. The name given to this courageous female was Franziska Mann.

When she was a child, Franziska Rosenberg (the ballerina's birth name) stood a high opportunity to be successful. She attended the private ballet academy Irena Prusik where the skills she learned were developed by highly regarded instructors. Their hard work was successful. In the final year of college, Franziska could perform dances in any direction, From classical to modern. She participated at the Brussels International Dance Competition, at which she was able to beat more than hundred competitors in the competition, she came 4th. Then, it seemed like she was a gifted dancer, she had promising prospects. But, then

September arrived and brought with it the Second World War. The lightning action that turned Poland as an independent country into a governorship subordinate to the general government of Germany. The advent of the Nazis and their pseudo-Christian ideology about Jews Jews brought Polish officials Polish officials of this group on the edge of their own survival.

The ones who weren't destroyed in the immediate aftermath of the German soldiers were classified in ghettos, which were specially identified areas, the income of which was pretty restricted, and earning cash for food. The most well-known of these Polish reservation - known as the Warsaw ghetto the ghetto was occupied by Franziska who, at the date was married, and was christened Mann.

The money she earned was from dancing in the Melody Palace cabaret theatre in the Ghetto. It was clear that she didn't have alternatives which is why she chose to do what she knew. The prospect of dying slowly within the reservations, and being almost in prison, wasn't enough for her so she searched for alternatives to alter her situation. A chance to change her position appeared to a lot of Warsaw Jews, appeared in 1942.

There was a rumor that began to circulate in the ghetto about the possibility that Jews with passports of an unfriendly country will be permitted to travel from the ghetto of Warsaw and go to another nation in exchange in exchange for the taken German military.

A lot of people who were searching at every opportunity to get out of that was warsaw and escape the ghetto of Warsaw reservation, did not realize that these stories began being circulated by co-laborer Jews who were part of The "Jagev" organization cooperating with the Nazis. They German co-conspirators were alleged to have "secretly" carried this information throughout the Ghetto area. In the end, Jews were aware of it as did the underground. They circulated it through their networks with the hopes that world Zionist groups can aid the plight of Warsaw Jews.

In fact, a few Jewish foundations that were based in Switzerland started to issue passports to Warsaw and other cities, which largely were issued by South American states. To avoid provoking suspicion from the local Jews as well as the global community, during the spring of 1943 they started making passports, not just as such, but also for cash, as well as very big ones. In the beginning, the value of the passports for saving was estimated to be equal to today's twenty thousand US dollars. It instantly stifled any chance of salvation for a majority of residents living in ghettos.

Alas! The scheme used was deceitful and cynical. It was a cynical deceit. Nazis were not thinking of pulling from captivity their soldiers, but they did they did, in a shrewd way of inducing a small number of Jews that were residing in Warsaw in the Ghetto. There were no options for the Warsaw Jews as well as in the regime of occupation, only a handful of individuals rushed out with the family's last jewelry, which was hidden as they said, "for extreme cases." One among them included Franziska Mann. As many other people were a believer in the "secret" rumors that Jews that can purchase a high-priced passport issued by South America South American state will be in a position to flee and leave Poland that was under the control of the Nazis.

The first time, everything went quite good for Francis. As did others "happy" owners of salvatory passports, moved into"Poland," a hotel "Poland", located in the "Aryan" part of the city. It was also the home of an organization that's primary task was to make arrangements the process for Jews to relocate to Warsaw in South Africa. Indeed, the whole operation was just one of the many productions the Germans were able to masterfully execute. The summer of 1943, police descended on the hotel, and made a selection of 300 guests. They were then sent for transport to in the French city of Vittel and were ensconced at an interment facility. The reason for this incident is to facilitate a swap to German prisoners.

If anyone stayed at the hotel, a new "program" was prepared. The announcement was that they would be transferred to a new location - the camp in

Burgau situated in the southern part of Germany. They are then transported into neutral Switzerland. The group that was involved in the group, which was 2.5-3 thousand persons, among which it was Franziska Mann.

They were all taken to the station, from where they were placed onto a train, which took out on a lengthy, journey, and as was revealed, most difficult journey. Many people were unaware the fact that, instead of South Germany they were being transferred to Auschwitz. Auschwitz death camp which was situated in Poland. On arrival at the final station at Auschwitz, the Jews were welcomed with Franz Hessler, who introduced himself as a representative in the Ministry of Foreign Affairs. However, this individual smiled warmly at people arriving as the leader of the guards at camp. He informed those who arrived in the stations that they were required to take certain formal steps to get across the border. The main reason was to shower and clean their the clothes. The bathroom was housed was just a few feet away to the station, and therefore all visitors needed to be there for quick completion of the formalities.

The building known as the shower was nothing more than an underground gas chamber. When the locker room was opened the people were greeted by a foul scent, and were told about an area in which Jews were burned and poisoned with real lines. Furthermore to that, the Germans who were accompanying them weren't so polite as the ones on the street. With the help of buttstocks and kicks, they forced the people into removing their belongings. They dispelled doubts about the unfortunate. But, even though there was absolutely no way to escape from the present situation Fraciska Mann was not accustomed to give up. So, she decided to make use of her last chance to fight.

The beautiful and young woman, in spite of the requests to expedite the process of removing her clothes started to perform exactly the opposite, in slow motion with the graceful elegance of an ballerina. The young SS males, who were paying close the attention of Francis, began to genuinely examine Francis. She then went to the entire dance and one at a time, taking off the details of her attire, slowly moving towards the guards. When she came close to one the guards, SS non-commissioned officer Emmerich She threw all the hatred she had accumulated into one strike by throwing high-heeled shoes at the face of Emmerich.

The stunned Nazi pulled out a gun to kill the angry Jew and did not anticipate the quick response of a professional dancer. The moment the German took the holster off, the dancer reached for a gun and fired a number of shots with the gun. Two rounds struck his companion Emmerich Josef Schillinger. He was a prison guard, who was renowned by his ferocity and sadistic tendencies towards prisoners. A second bullet smashed Emmerich's knee. Sounding shots signalled to the rest of the ladies in the gym. They instantly rushed towards the heavy-armed guards hoping to cause the greatest harm on the guards.

The fact is that male strength, augmented by the shooting of guns, prevailed the day. The wounded and dead guards and their wounded companions managed to get out of the area, while the women themselves were confined to the room. Following that, the chief of the Sonderkommando instructed to shoot all directly through the walls of the structure, rather than stop a riot that was brewing. The orders were immediately carried out.

Camp commander Rudolf Hess reported his incident to his superiors. The exact names of the people who participated in the event were announced through Adolf Eichmann, who spoke about this incident at the hearing. Additional details about the women's protest in the midst of the chamber not as significant. What is important here is that the woman who was a fragile an actress from Warsaw who had no intention of doing so she became an emblem of unwavering resistance to the total evil. Her actions showed everyone that even with no chance to fight, the ultimate struggle is for the righteous to die. Then Francis Mann won it for absolutely.

War and love the romance between the victim and her rescuer

Edith Steiner and John MacKay

They remained in contact for 71 years, both the victim and her liberator: Jewish woman Edith Steiner as well as Scotsman John MacKay. Edith was imprisoned at Auschwitz. Her journey to Auschwitz's death camp together with her mother. They stayed there an indefinitely for about a month and a half. Both of them had a good luck. There was no one else in the Steiner family did survive. The entire family was destroyed by the chamber of gas.

Edith's fate Edith may be different, too. Edith was sent to Auschwitz right at the moment the Doctor. Death - Mengele - was carrying out his inhumane tests on humans. He personally met with each group, bringing an entire new batch of prisoners as well as conducted an examination of the prisoners, separating them in "workers" and "animals" to conduct his brutal tests. Edith as well as her mother were taken to labor slaves.

Tired and exhausted from the effects of hunger and dehydration, the soldiers were exhausted as the allied forces retreated into the suburbs of Auschwitz. The most notable member of those in the Scottish commando assault team who also played a part in liberating the biggest concentration camp in Europe included John MacKay. He was aware of the plight of being held in captivity as well as slavery. When he was at the start of war was seized by Italians however, he was able to escape after taking on the uniforms that he was wearing as the Italian soldier.

Thus, with intense feelings that he conveyed his weapons his freedom to prisoner of Auschwitz. John was a hero soldier, and when he was in combat was unflinching in his fight. However, when he came across Edith He was humiliated when he was a kid. First time, she was seen inside a prison cell. Her eyes were huge and appeared more expansive because her face was slim. The second time, they came together was at the liberation celebration.

John was so eager to dance with a gorgeous Jewish woman, however, he was hesitant to meet her. He then John invited his friend to the girl, and offered to dance. The girl was shocked by this stifling attitude and responded that she'd be dancing happily in the event that John himself had asked her. He did. The dance was the deciding factor in their future. MacKay brought the bride as well as the mother of her to Scotland to marry her. In June of 1946, they got married. They had a great life and managed to keep their friendship throughout their times of conflict and pain. They had two kids as well as five grandchildren and seven great-grandchildren. Edith is now 92 older, while John has reached 96. they're still very happy.

Happily married couple, the victim and her salvation

The amazing story of Alice the princess

Alice

with her son. Alice along with her young son

It was a remarkable feat that Princess Alice, the mom of prince Philip, princess Alice of Battenberg was able to protect the Jewish family despite the connections to the royal family of her own family that was in the upper levels within the Nazi party. The princess Alice was born in England in the year 1885. She is an ancestor of queen Victoria. Her father was the son of a German prince as was her mother, a

British princess. Alice was part of the majority of royal families across Europe. Alice was also different from other women in her singularity.

In the age of eight years old, Alice was diagnosed with hearing loss, and Alice was able to discern lips. Then, a few family members speculated that the deafness of her mother led Alice to be more aware of the struggles of other people and more tolerant to individuals who were not part of society.

Alice discovered her love for Andrew, who was at the time Prince Andrew, the Prince of Greece, Andrew, during the coronation ceremony of her cousin Edward VII, the Prince Edward VII, in London in 1902. Following that year, they got married. The couple was blessed with one daughter Philip as well as four girls. The princesses Alice along with Prince Andrew were acquaintances with Haymaki ("Haim")

Cohen known as a prominent Jewish politician in the Greek Parliament, along with his wife Rachel as well as their families. As they became aware of the growing anti-Semitism across Europe the royal family vowed to assist the Cohens should they required assistance. The time of peace for the nation came to an end in 1921. The Greek Revolution forced the royal family to move to Paris.

In Paris in the 1920s, Prince Andrew was able to divorce his wife, and retreated into the world of a reckless drinker. Alice was devastated and even ended up in an psychiatric institution for two years during the 1930s. Following her hospitalization her return to Athens in her own. The son Philip was placed in a home in a variety of family members. Then, the cousin of Philip remembered that, when the prince came to visit the family for Christmas and enrolled in the guestbook of his family and provided the address of his residence as "without a certain place of residence". The four daughters of Alice got married German Aristocrats.

As World War II broke out and the war broke out, prince Philip was a volunteer to join the British navy. There, he bravely served in the battles. The princesses' lives differed greatly: the couples of all four princesses held high positions within their respective positions in the Nazi government. One daughter, Princess Margaret, and her husband, Prince Gottfried of Hohenlohe-Langenburg, rebelled against Hitler. Prince Gottfried was planning to commit the assassination of Hitler during 1944, but the plot was discovered before the plot could be executed. Three daughters from Alice were fervent Nazis. One of them even gave her son the name Carl Adolf in honor of Adolf Hitler.

With the approaching war, Haymaki Cohen and his family began to be in greater danger. In 1941, when Germany began to invade Greece in 1941 in 1941, the Cohens moved to Athens in Athens, which was under Italian administration and regarded as an area that was safer to live for Jews in comparison to areas that were under German government. The situation changed dramatically after September 1943 after which Germany assumed control over Athens and began to hunt for Jews with the intention of removal. In 1943 Haymaki Cohen passed to death and his family was looking desperately for options to get out of Greece. One of his children went to Cairo to be a part of the Greek government, but the remainder of the Cohen family was still in Athens.

In the wake of their situation, Alice sent a message to Rachel, the mother of Haymaki, Rachel, that she was prepared to protect their entire family. Rachel as well as Tilde, her daughter Tilde agreed to the suggestion from Alice and relocated, then their son Michel was also a part of the family. The time was when Alice had recently relocated from her humble home to an even bigger house that was belonging to her son-in law who looked after the home. The house was large enough to provide Alice with ample space to provide an adequate shelter for her family. The main problem was the house was only a couple of meters away from the main office of the Gestapo located in Athens. In some instances there were instances when the Gestapo believed that the queen of Athens was guilty of anti-Nazi activities, and dragged her into interrogation. When this happened, Alice pretended not to be able to answer their questions due to her hearing loss.

A trusted acquaintance Alice DeMosen Puri recalled the times of war: "The Princess gave Mrs. Cohen and her daughter (and afterward her son) the apartment they needed, a tiny two-room one located on the third first floor ... The group of individuals who knew about this was confined to methe queen who was the sole authorized to go visit the Cohens family and a handful of committed princesses. Through these lengthy and challenging moments, I visited the home of Mrs. Cohen and her children at home, assisted the family stay in touch with the world around them as well as carried out numerous chores, and attempted to cheer them up and never let them lose their heart.

In the midst of a difficult time in those years of struggle, Brothers Alice the Lord of Britain Monbatten, had the ability to get food items in packages to her sister. In the event of receiving these parcels, Alice distributed them to the poor.

Alice did not tell her family about her bravery which was destined to discover the story in the years following the war had ended. The year 1993 was the time when "Yad Vashem" posthumously granted the princess the honourary the title "Righteous Among the Nations" for her role in sheltering and helping those in the Cohens family. While it was true that the British royal family was never allowed to make an official visit to Israel, in 1993 the Jewish state, prince Philip and his younger sister Margarita was invited to Israel to witness a special ceremony to honor his mother.

Chapter 4: Queen Elizabeth and Prince Philip

Prince Philip put up a plant to honor the memories of his mother and delivered a heartfelt speech.

"The Holocaust was the most horrible event that has occurred in the time of Jewish people. It will be remembered in the hearts of future generations. The burial of thousands of non-Jews as my mother was as well as those who felt the grief and pain of those who suffered and made every effort to ease the pain of all the victims was a admirable action. My mother did not realize that what she did was special. "

Prince Philip stated: "She would consider this a completely natural human reaction towards people in distress."

Teacher's praise Jeanne Daman

Jeanne Daman

There is not much information concerning Jeanne Daman. There are no books written about her, and none of the films has been produced. However, many people continue to express their gratitude to her for saving the life of Jewish children she helped in World War II. Jeanne Daman was born and resided in Belgium. Daman was unaware about the daily life of Jews and was far from the issues they faced until beginning of the war. Belgium was among the very few countries in Europe that refused to accept Nazism. The atrocities perpetrated in other nations were and not just by Germans and also the people living there, but in Belgium this was the job mostly by the Nazis.

As an example, nobody other than the chief of the government that was occupying, Wehrmacht General personally participated in the rescue of Jewish children. The director of the Belgian Department of Education was required to sign a law prohibiting Jewish students from attending the same institution as other students as well as immediately taking part in the establishing of Jewish kindergartens and schools. He also participated in and bringing the most renowned Belgian teachers to these establishments.

Chaim Perelman is a Professor of law and logic of the University of Belgium, goes underground and supplies those working underground with fake documents that claim to be from Jews who are of non-Jewish descent. Perelman has been asked step down and resign, however he does not write a formal statement. Are you sure Perelman was shot or jailed because of the incident? Not at all. He was able to keep his job and income, but was instructed not to deliver lectures. The vast majority of Belgian citizens were peacefully protesting against the actions of the government in occupation.

Maybe that's an explanation for why some of the largest struggles of underground workers took place in Belgium.

Jeanne Daman at first had absolutely nothing to do with the underground resistance group. Her job was to run an educational center to Jews as a teacher, and even though she was Belgian was quick to agree.

The year was 1942. Jeanne could organize the work efficiently. But, she quickly recognized that she would not be working in the school for a long time. As the first arrests began of Jews in the city, she started to contact families on a daily basis to inquire why this child or another stopped school. Her answers were shocking. Arrests!

In the meantime, friends and neighbors started to take children to Jeanne's kindergarten that were sent to the kindergarten without parents at all since they were detained. Some parents, concerned that Nazis could be coming after their children They began to request Jeanne to hide their children in a safe place.

Then came the actual secret operation that was the work of Jeanne Daman. Her school was shut down the preschool and was involved in organizing a place to hide for the children. At first, she reached out to Yvon Nevyan, an eminent underground worker from Brussels who assisted Jeanne to transport the children to Belgian orphanages. After that, Fela Perelman assisted in contacting the monasteries. Children started to seek refuge there. The burgomaster of Brussels commune Ukkel was also responsible for the protection of dozens of Jewish youngsters. Then, all of the children in the Jewish kindergarten were able to stay within safe areas.

There were times when it was possible to aid adults. Professor Perelman provided fake papers, as well as some women had the opportunity to serve as maids or service workers to wealthy Belgian residences and they could hide Jewish women in the area.

When Jeanne was able to recognize each of her wards Fela Perelman asked Jeanne to ask for help in getting other kids out, but not school. and Jeanne was quick to agree without hesitation. In accordance with all laws of the conspiracy, she sat at the bus station and was waiting for the child to come into her sight unnoticed. After that, she grabbed him by her hand, and then led him away to him, or took him away. generally, she just hid the child inside a secure place.

Following the release from Belgium, Jeanne Daman took over the reunion of dispersed families. Over the course of a year she devoted herself to searching for children, and then determining the future for their families. It was a joy to watch mothers, following the long time of separation, suffering and agony, real pain as well as all the trauma she endured hugging and pressing her child's heart into her chest!

A few days later, members from the underground asked Jeanne to ask for assistance in finding names of collaborators serving the government of fascism. Jeanne agreed. Jeanne accepted. Once she donned the uniform she became a member of the German group "Winter Aid" and quickly gained the trust of its members. She began compiling list of collaborators, and then pass these lists for the Belgium underground resistance group. They also passed on other classified information to the partisans. She even handed them weapons close to the conclusion of the conflict.

A lot of the children that were that were saved by Joan didn't have their parents around for a long time. The main concern of Jeanne Daman was to find new homes that would take care of them, or finding close friends, relatives or family members, who would accept to be an orphanage family. Jeanne Daman was not at peace until she had arranged the destiny of her children.

Then, in 1946 Jeanne Daman marries a professor at an American university before moving to the USA. The truth is that, in America, she continues to help the Jews. United States, she continues helping those who are Jews. Jeanne starts fundraising for the newly established Jewish state. Later, to honor of her husband, the literature professor Aldo Scaglione established The

Aldo Scaglione and Jeanne Scaglione award.

Albert Einstein himself presented her with a picture of appreciation for what the fragile young woman had done to help Jewish children in the post-war period. In addition "Yad Vashem" assigned Jeanne Daman the title "Righteous Among the Nations". Her name is on the tree and her name is growing along the Alley of the Righteous since the year 1971.

The concert that ended the career of Musya Pinkenzon.

Eleven year old violinist Musya Pinkenzon

The violinist of 11 years old did not shoot a single soldier of the enemy however, he made his mark on the course of conflict as a hero. He was a fighter against Nazism for just a few seconds, but he was able to teach an example of bravery to numerous individuals. The full name of the Jewish child was Abram Pinkenzon. He is, however, better known as Musya. Mother Fenya Moiseevna gently addressed her son.

Musya is born the 5th of December 1930 within the "Traditional Jewish family", in the time in the city of Balti and was later affixed to Romania. The Pinkenzons belonged the doctor dynasty, that was comprised of multiple generations. The family's head, Vladimir, became a well-known doctor who was highly valued by his patients. He was not surprised to see that his son was the future of his company. The attraction to music was more intense. An exceptionally talented boy, by age five was able to master the violin. He was proficient at playing the musical instrument. His talent was reported even in the local newspapers.

In the year 1940, Balti as a part of Bessarabia was admitted to into the Soviet state. The Pinkenzons didn't really experience any changes. Vladimir was still practicing medicine while his son, who was a member of into the Soviet Pioneers organization, was immersed in music. In June 1941, he was planning to address the First amateur Olympiad of Moldova. The beginning of the Great Patriotic War destroyed the peace talks.

The Pinkenzons began to evacuate. In the course of a couple of months, they reached the Kuban (region located in Southern Russia) Village in Ust-Labinsk. The family's head started working at a military hospital. His son was enrolled in an elementary school in the area and stay in the hospital during evening hours performing entertainment for wounded soldiers using the violin.

The Germans advanced rapidly and during the summer of 1942, the Kuban was in danger too. There was a need to evacuate the injured as well as medical personnel, however the local Soviet officials did not have the sufficient time for this. The doctor Dr. Vladimir Pinkenzon continued to take care of his patients until Nazis arrested his clinic. When they learned that he was a an extremely well-respected and highly trained physician, they asked Pinkenzon to help in the care for those German soldiers. But, Pinkenzon refused them, and was sent to jail. Within a couple of days the spouse and son also were in prison. The fascists did not think only to eliminate the Jews who resided in the community, but also to carry out an act of terror against other individuals.

Everyone in Ust-Labinsk were led to the spot of execution. The condemned were able to see Musya Pinkenzon, who could not let go of his primary instrument, which he and was gently placed on his chest. Within the crowd, the phrase "inhuman" was heard. Vladimir requested the German policeman not to shoot the child, but he the boy was killed immediately. The wife of the deceased, Fenya Moiseevna who was quick to comfort her deceased husband's grave, was killed shortly thereafter. The 11-year-old with whom the Nazis murdered the most close persons to him, remained in a solitary place among the "true Aryans," who thought of him as an "subhuman." The fear and the despair were on the souls of all those in the lines of Nazis and who were unable to help Musya.

Chapter 5: The last photo of the hero boy

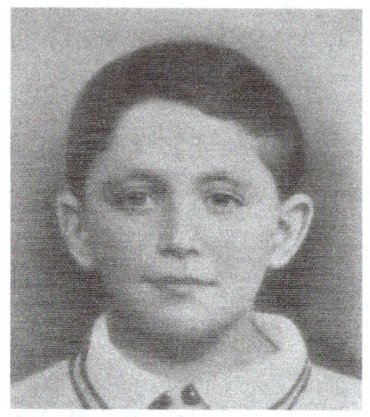

Suddenly, the child demanded the officer to meet the last wish of his - perform the violin. Officer laughed at him and then gave permission. The officer probably believed that the small Jew tried to soothe him, and plead for more moments of his life.

A moment later after that, music was heard over the town. There was no panic, nor the Nazis initially seemed to be aware, and possibly, they were not able to comprehend that something was taking place. Then Musya who was gazing into the death's eyes performed her rendition of the "International", which at the time, was not just the national anthem for communists across the globe and also the USSR. People in the crowd began to sing quietly beginning, became louder and louder, singing an anthem to the beat of the instrument of the little Jewish boy.

The officer who was awakened, having declared the child to be as a pig, and shouting with a loud voice, ordered the child to cease his performance right away. Nazi soldiers started firing at the musician. The wounded Musya was able to carry on playing however the rumbling bullets halted the performance of the player. The Nazis raged at the masses, chasing them away out of rage. The deeds were done in the form of intimidation, as conceived by Nazis was the cause of humiliation. The

Nazis did not have a chance against the courage of a 11 year old Jewish boy who had no fear of dying. It was a pivotal moment for inhabitants of Ust-Labinsk. Faith in the victory against the fascists thanks to the courageous little singer ignited their hearts by a fresh force.

The city of Ust-Labinsk the monument of an actual hero, a an aspiring violinist Musya Pinkenzon has been constructed, who's fight against Nazism took just a few seconds, and then became an icon of determination and courage.

The Bielski Brothers' tale

Bielski brothers Tuvia, Asael and Zus

Bielski brothers were part of the partisan group that was the largest and most effective partisan group during WW II, which had more than 750 Jewish combatants in 1943. It was founded in Belarus. The origins of four Belsky brothers four brothers namely Tuvia, Asael, Zus and Aron from the partisans' group was so dramatic, that numerous books, documentaries and films were devoted to the story of their group.

The Bielski family included 12 children including 10 boys and 2 girls. They resided in Poland. They owned a piece of agricultural land, and youngest son, Tuvia, owned a tiny store. Tuvia attended a Jewish religious Jewish school and later studying in Polish. He spoke six languages, Yiddish, Russian, Belarusian, Polish, Hebrew and German. He was a member of his unit in the Polish Army and was promoted to the rank of corporal. In the aftermath of Soviet invasion in Poland The Bielski family were made Soviet citizens.

In the days prior to the German attack against the USSR in the early days of the war, it was the Soviet secret police held an event to find the socially affluent and then remove them from Siberia. Tuvia who was the store's owner of the business, fell under this classification. The store became nationalized after the war, Tuvia left a small town in which the store was located, and moved to a different location. The two brothers he had as younger Asael as well as Zus were drafted into join the Red Army.

Following the assault on Belarus by Germans in summer 1941, and the massacre of the Jewish populace, Two from Bielski Brothers, Jacob and Abraham Bielski Brothers, Jacob and Abraham were killed at by Nazis. Then, on December 7, 1941, the parents and youngest sister from the Bielski family and Zus's wife as well as their infant daughter were all shot by the local Jews. Aron, the younger brother of 12 years old, miraculously avoided dying and joined his older brothers.

The brothers were able to get to the forests a group of relatives that formed the foundation of the upcoming Jewish group of guerrillas. In the beginning, there were only 17 individuals in the team as well as a pistol that had inadequate ammunition. Tuvia Bielski was chosen as the commanding officer.

As of August, 1942 the group increased to 250 members who were Novogrudok exiles from the ghetto. The autumn of 1942 was when the Bielski team began to engage in combat and gaining respect from Partisans. Tuvia Bielski established himself as an experienced and determined leader. It played an important role in the recognition that was given to the Bielski team of partisans by top leaders of the Soviet political movement.

Tuvia, who was fluent in many languages and could pass as a non-Jew. He often was a fugitive in the Jewish Ghetto to persuade those in the ghetto to leave towards the forest. Tuvia was a friend to everyone who was Jews as well as women, those over 65 and even children. The detachment, however, was a ferocious combat unit that everybody was required to face with: the Germans as well as the Soviet Partisans, and the rest of the people.

Tuvia Bielski believed that the primary goal of her mission to save the lives of the most Jews as it was feasible. In spite of his hatred of the Nazis and the Nazis, the Bielski brothers acted on the premise that "it is better to save one old Jewish woman than to kill ten German soldiers." They represented a village that was dubbed "Forest Jerusalem". It had an artisan bakery, forge, a tannery the bathhouse, a hospital and a primary school. The village also included cooks, musicians, potters and tailors. Weddings even took place at the supper club, run by Rabbi David Brook.

The squad members were housed in dugouts. The ones who weren't active in battle were able to repair weapons, sew clothing and offered other support to Soviet militants. They were provided with medication, ammunition, and food rather. The Bielski team of bombers was regarded as one of the top people to sabotage and had a lot of respect by those who were members of the partisans.

In the spring of 1943, the size of the unit reached 750 members. The relations with other partisans were never good. To offend the those who were part of the Belsky team was not an option that they could take the guns and put in over a hundred soldiers who were ready to protect their own people against any intrusions.

The most significant issue was producing food to feed many individuals. Peasants started to work with the guerrillas once they realized that Bielski wasn't a target to be hunted. If a peasant from the area gave Nazis an entire group of Jews and they seized the house, the avengers of Bielski's squad Bielski team destroyed the house and the entire family. They also burnt the house of Informer. Later on, the Bielski squad Bielski was famous because they took on the task of punishing collaborators. According to the words from the residents, a large number of victims were treated with respect.

Some guerrilla groups were hesitant to welcome Jews who had fled the ghetto which was why they were turned back to be executed or killed. For the Jews, the only hope for Jews was the detachment of Tuvia Bielski.

The Germans assaulted the camp a few times, but the troops retreated and resisted with an fighting with guns. The largest anti-partisan campaign "Herman", which began on July 15th, 1943, the group relocated to a tiny island located in the swamp. There, the Germans did not manage to capture the group.

The squad then was split into family and combat sections. The camp for family members, comprised the time, around 700 individuals. It was situated deep in the forests in Belarus and was commanded by Tuvia Bielski. They were under direction of Zus who was later transferred into the area of Stankevichej and Asael was the head of the department for intelligence.

The most brutal of attack teams endured on the day of Belarus' liberation. Belarus. On the 9th of July 1944, the retreating German elements engaged in a battle with the rebels. Dozens of victims were injured 9 people were killed. Later that day, they Red Army entered the area of forest, in which the group was hiding.

They Bielski brothers' party team were able to protect them from their destruction 1230 Jews. The Bielski brothers all endured the siege and waited to see the release from Belarus through the Red Army. In the midst of it all, Tuvia was taken to Minsk in which he wrote an exhaustive report of the work of his group.

According to the Professor of the history department David Melzer, the squad "has derail 6 echelons of the enemy and pushed them into the front lines, blowing up 20 highway and railway bridges, fought 12 in ambushes and open combats as well as destroyed 16 cars, and a live force more than 250 German officers and soldiers. "Zus Bielski was the only person to destroy 47 Nazis and their collaborators. To honor the leader of Tuvia Bielski Tuvia Bielski, Germans awarded a prize of 100,000 Reichsmarks!

Hollywood filmmaker Edward Zwick made movie "Defiance" Based on the amazing account of the three Bielski brothers.

Chapter 6: The History of the Second World War

The argument has been made it was this First World War set the conditions for the subsequent war because it created instability within Europe. In the end, Second World War proved to be the most gruelling conflict ever. The rising of Adolf Hitler in Germany stirred the conflict on numerous fronts. Hitler was elected to power during in a period in which the politics and economy of Germany did not seem to be stable. Along together with the Nazi group, Hitler made pacts in a deliberate manner with Italy as well as Japan and aimed to rule the globe, thus proving that Germany was superior to other German populace. The attack on Poland the territory allies had sworn to protect in 1939, prompted both the French as well as the British to declare the war against Germany and mark the start of the Second World War. The war would finish taking more lives, degrading property and land with lasting effects on the lives of survivors and generations that come. The conflict that lasted for 6 years was the longest and most destructive one in the history of wars across the globe. The figures of those killed during battle was sixty to 80 million. In addition to the deaths, staggering six million Jews suffered in Nazi concentration camps in the course of Hitler's infamous "Final Solution," now called the Holocaust.

Following are some of the major moments of the Second World War:

The Clash Near the Marco Polo Bridge (7 July 1937)

The first phase of the full-on conflict in the region between Japan and China began with an unimaginable fight between Japanese teams participating in an exercise for military near the Marco Polo

Bridge, southwest of Beijing. The Japanese believed that their honour was being questioned and challenged which led to them sending a contingent of soldiers to the area. Despots within the Japanese army profited from the situation to demand China to settle the matter to their advantage. But the Chinese leaders, who were pro-independence, Jiang Jieshi, refused to accept requests of Japanese. At the end of the day, the brawl erupted in a tense manner and weakened both the Japanese as well as the Chinese completely. At the close of July, an extensive dispute broke out leading to the invasion and annexation in Beijing in the hands of Japanese.

Germans' Offensives to the West (10 May 1940)

The dictatorship of Hitler's Germany was unable to restrain their offensive following the attack on Poland. His inability to participate in powerful negotiations and agreements also resulted in the spreading of war into different parts of the globe. The victory over Poland gave Germany an advantage in fighting in the same front. This was a reason for Hitler to prompt his troops to advance to the west, saying that Germany had more experience in the battle than the other countries, either France or Britain. Hitler needed to postpone his attacks from 1 May 1940. This was due to extreme weather conditions in Germany during 1940.

In addition, there were numerous instructions from the top commander of Germany in reference to the necessity of a proper preparation. This prevented the attack from going ahead. The attack of France came after the accusations. The unexpected attack worked because Britain as well as France did not have to form a unified defense. In the following 7 weeks,

Germany lead a battle to change the face of Europe through the acquisition of vast areas. This victory strengthened Hitler's faith of his inevitable success.

A Look at the Battle of Britain

The collapse of France enabled Germany to invade the borders of Britain in the 12th august 1940 the very first intense assault against the airfields in Britain was launched. Hitler ordered his German military to remove the British warships out of the channel to make space for the next attacks to come. The Luftwaffe (air forces) commanders were becoming increasingly anxious about initiating an attack against the RAF and other structures in order to prepare for an imminent attack. The air force instead attempted to make Britain to surrender by bombardment war against civilian targets, a plan of attack that would place the air force at the frontline.

The Battle of Britain was the largest historical war to be waged in the air was fought when the German air forces engage in a number of air attacks at Britain's defence forces. But, the RAF won the conflict at the close in October, 1940. The German soldiers were not able to organize their air assault as well as the land invasion cropping unit, resulting in their defeat during the Battle of Britain. Furthermore they Germans did not have strategic air offensive groups. In contrast they had British were able to demonstrate superior ground control and radar systems, a crucial element in their victory in the conflict.

Operation Barbarossa (22 June 1941)

After victories over Poland, Belgium, and the Netherlands, Hitler grew overconfident. He began to dislike different political systems and wished to kill their government to gain the freedom he long for. The desire to attack to the Soviet Union grew. Hitler became more worried regarding the plans of Stalin and concluded that conflict with communists was inevitable. The delusions of Stalin led to Hitler the conviction that a war against the Soviet Union would be straightforward. Thus, he received an array of erroneous military intelligence and estimates of the size of the army of the Red and the potential for mobilization of their forces. Hitler believed that the defeat of the Soviet Union would make Britain accept Germany's control of Europe. That belief pushed Hitler to initiate the military operation "Barbarossa," his biggest failure in the war. On the 22nd of June, German forces launched an unexpected attack against the Soviet Union. They did not have a program. The end result was that Germany was dragging itself into a conflict that could eventually end in loss.

The Attack on Pearl Harbor (7 December 1941)

The attack was viewed as an obvious military action In what was seen as a clear act of war, the Japanese struck the home of the American Pacific Fleet at Pearl Harbor on the island of Oahu within the Hawaiian archipelago. The Japanese considered the attack to be an opportunity to warn America to United States to stop opposing the expansionist strategy of Japan. The Japanese planned to destroy the whole American Pacific Fleet. This strategy could be seen as an operational victory from one end, but an operational disaster in the opposite.

The destruction to American battleships in Pearl Harbor forced the Americans to focus more on more effective naval planning. The Americans were more focused on the three vessels that weren't present in the moment of the assault (the

Lexington, the Yorktown as well as Enterprise). Enterprise). Because of the focus on taking down the battleships, and but not their equipment or installation and installation, the assault on Pearl Harbor remained the most important attack against any naval fleet during the course of conflict.

In the course of war, weaknesses in the strategy concepts that governed the Japanese strategies were exposed. The first was that the Japanese were not aware of the power of money in the United States and the resolve of its citizens. Second they Japanese were too eager to start an offensive which was not needed.

But the huge size of the Japanese battleships, particularly the cruisers and carriers, would be compared to American fleets of Pearl Harbor. The bombing of Pearl Harbor marked the official arrival into American forces into U.S. in the Second World War.

Battle of Midway (4 June 1942)

The power of the American navy was demonstrated at midway in the Battle of Midway during the battle of midway, in which Americans won. This battle also demonstrated the power of American research and repair capabilities due to attacks (by Japanese). Japanese). Coordination of American carriers and bombers was essential in the war.

As the Americans were becoming more organized when it came to handling uncertainty, the Japanese weren't sure of which strategies to use. The Japanese were faced with the challenge of having to decide whether they would make their planes ready for landing or ship targets, a source of worry that delayed battle.

The capacity for the Americans to gain knowledge from their experience during the battle for the Coral Sea and the reliance on their strategic skills was crucial in the fight. The Americans depended on two men to identify Japanese enemies. The Japanese were unable to defend themselves against the assaults of the American dive-bombers. This was just a minor incident of coordination that failed.

The attack changed the size of carrier power across the Pacific. Within a short time it was clear that the Japanese had a shortage of highly trained and aggressive soldiers to patrol the oceans. It was difficult to replace lost pilots and not the least because of the lack of fuel to run the exercises. Four carriers were lost maintenance teams was a significant setback to efforts by the Japanese to take the fight.

The Japanese had to abandon all of their heavy transporters which led to the victory by the United States in the battle. At the end of the day, it was the American carrier strategy was portrayed in the form of a "lack-of-battleship" strategy.

Battle of Kursk (5 July 1943)

It was regarded as the most significant attack ever initiated by the Germans in the Eastern Front. The Germans decided to take advantage of the possibilities provided by the crucial German strategic. Hitler turned to tactical analysis, seeing the war as a complete extinction was his own to conquer (he thought he was the best). Hitler believed that a victory this battle would be demoralizing for the allies and reduce their belief that they could achieve Soviet victory. But, the Germans were outnumbered due to the high-tech nature that was the Soviet defense system that thwarted every German offensives.

The Germans lost a lot and were forced by Hitler to stop the attack. The retreat of German forces enabled the Soviets to counterattack, pushing the Germans away.

The D-Day (6 June 1944)

The D-Day is the date of landing for the Allied Forces in northern France started on June 6th, 1944. The day that D-Day began, American, British, and Canadian troops landed in Normandy. The Allied forces had planned the landing (referred as the operation 'Neptune') and the invasion of the area (termed the operation "Overload"). They were successful due to the organized and well-organized naval support to the air strike. Furthermore the Allied were successful in deceiving the enemy, Operation 'Fortitude' which took the Normandy off guard.

This was due to the Germans focus on defenses and their forces within their

Calais region. The Calais region offered a comparatively tiny sea crossing, and an easier way towards Germany. In contrast it was also the case that Normandy was accessible via the ports of assault along the southern shores of England (particularly ports like Plymouth, Portland, and Portsmouth). In addition there was the issue that the Germans were not equipped with enough naval weapons as well as human resources to stop the Annexation.

The German commandos often were in disagreement over the best strategy to follow. In many instances they could not agree on the most appropriate method to respond. Surprisingly, leaders were not united on important decision-making. Some wanted to move German 10 panzer divisions closer near the coastline to take on the allies prior to being able to establish a permanent base. A different group tried to preserve the divisions as reserves to be used for strategic purposes during the time of war. Failure to establish a system for making decisions caused an unrest between the German groups.

The landing was a variety of shapes. For example the British created separate tanks that could be used to take on coastal defenses. In particular, the vessels of Crab-wave for the attack on minefields at Gold, Juno, and Sword beaches. The plan worked. The Allied troops (Canadians as well as British) which were on the beach took positions of cover as a strategy to fight German troops. German soldiers.

In contrast to their Canadian as well as British counterparts in the battle, American force that made it to the Omaha beach failed to implement the best war strategies. Their troubles began with a mistakenly launched assault, called the Duplex drive that came in a far distance from the beach. The American forces also didn't make use of the specially-designed arsenal during the assault. In the aftermath, Americans suffer massive injuries due to the failure to land and from those on the sides of the cliffs, which were not well-bludgeoned by the bombs.

But, the Americans were able to leap over into the huddle, and then march towards. After D-Day the jump-off point did not have enough depth which exposed the troops the risk of a German attack. The Americans had, nonetheless, blessed in that Germans did not have enough armor to be able to respond. The inability of the Germans to respond revealed the inelasticity that was caused by the interference of Hitler.

Operation Overload was an important step forward in battles on land and at sea, because the requirement to seize a port in order to land, strengthen and aid the invading forces was not required.

Allies did not intend to take over the ports which was a disappointment to the Germans with conflicting expectations. The plan of attack was well-organized. attack worked in the favor of allies. They laid pipelines for oil under the channel in order to keep supplies.

The tactics used during the battles proved extremely difficult for Allied forces to get through the Normandy (although they were successful throughout August).

Battle of Leyte Gulf (23-26 October 1944)

In the middle of October 1944, in mid-October 1944, the United States took advantage of the strength and expansion of its military and air force in order to start an assault to retake the Philippines. This led to the commencement of Battle of Leyte Gulf--the most epic battle on the seas in the Second World War. It was the U.S. used the fight to establish naval supremacy throughout the Western Pacific.

The actions of American force in the Philippines provided a number of difficulties for the Japanese. Conscient of the imminent loss, Japanese naval leaders objected to being beaten honorably. On October 18, 1944, the commander of the Naval Operations Section requested that the Japanese fleets be regarded by the Japanese Navy as "a fitting place to die" and given "the chance to bloom as flowers of death."

The Japanese used their fleets as bait to entice American carriers from the shores of the Philippines during an attack known"Sho-Go' (the victory of the victor). They used two striking navy forces to take on the weak American fleet. American fleet. The complicated scheming employed by the Japanese made it difficult for them to understand and handled properly by American leaders.

The Japanese almost offered a tangible form of opposition when they approached their Allies' landing area. They were Japanese striking force better than the Americans and was unable to strike. The strike force was retreated because they did not have the necessary naval expertise to discern the location of vessels of enemy. This inexperience triggered losing the Japanese by the Americans. The American forces took out four Japanese carriers and three battleships (including the Musashi) and ten cruisers, warships of other types, and even aircraft.

The Second Atomic Bomb Dropped on Japan (9 August 1945)

The second nuclear blast dropped in Nagasaki from The United States was more effective than the one dropped in Hiroshima. This attack showed that America was prepared to begin an unstoppable bombardment process. The attack destroyed an area of around seven kilometers in area to ashes. It killed over seventy-three thousand, injured over seventy-four thousand with long-lasting health effects.

The result was that Japan was compelled to give up its independence without condition. The 15th of August 1945 was the day that an imperial announcement declared the end of the wars after Emperor Hirohito's participation in the Imperial Conference on 9 and 14 August.

Chapter 7: The Holocaust

The term "Holocaust," derived from the Greek expression "holokaustos" (whole burnt sacrifice) is a term used historically as a reference to a burnt offering. In Hebrew the meaning of "Holocaust" was much more than just that. Some parts of it referred to it by the words "catastrophe" or "destruction." Since after the Great War, the term has been applied to the mass murder of over six million Jewish individuals, which included girls and women through the Nazis. The Nazis described the massacre as "the final solution" to the Jewish problems. The guiding force was Adolf Hitler, the anti-Semitic Nazis saw Jews as a weak race. Jews as being a minority that represented a danger to German health and well-being of the ethnic group as well as society overall. Mass prosecution of Jews in the context of Hitler's ultimate solution strategy which was carried out in concentration camps in Poland and in the current Holocaust.

Through time, artists have formulated terms to define the Holocaust. Raul Hilberg described the Holocaust as "the destruction of Jews of European origin," as Lucy S. Dawidowicz termed it "the war against the Jews." Others have depicted through their work, through film and writing what the Nazis made use of World War II to wage an ethnic war against Jews. The expression "Holocaust" has been used throughout history to describe the massacre of Jews. It is used in response to a definitive display of the slaughter in select extermination camps where the corpses of victims were burnt in open flames.

Before the Nazis took over the presidency in 1933, they already had let their resentment towards the Jews be known. At the time of 1919 Adolf Hitler had written his memoir, titled Mein Kampf (My Struggle) A controversial and controversial book, it was openly pro-Semitic in its views. The goal of the book was to inspire to the Nazis to "clear" all the Jews to make way for pure Germans. My Struggle was also an attempt to portray Jews as a "weak race" and Jews as being a "weak race" who were expected to be eliminated. In the initial Volume, Hitler posited that the elimination of a sick and weak race would be more compassionate than their security. In addition, Hitler observed that the elimination of "the weak and sick race" will create more room to "the strong." With the help of his illusions The Nazis created two major notions: greater Lebensraum (living spaces) that called for an expansion of the territorial space, as well as German power of the ethnic group.

Mein Kampf

Mein Kampf Mein Kampf was the book that revolutionized the Nazis views on Jews as well as accelerated Hitler's rise.

At the beginning of his rise to the rise of Hitler He maintained his fervent dislike of Jews, and blamed them for the majority of difficulties which Germany was facing. While prisoner, Hitler was able to come up with the idea of writing down his ideas, thoughts, and ideas for a future Germany on the form of a piece of paper. So, he began creating his memoir.

Some would say that Hitler composed the book My Struggle (translated). But the reality is that he never wrote it. In fact, Hitler dictated his thoughts to Rudolf Hess in his prison cell and afterward, at Berchtesgaden.

The reading of the Mein Kamp brings an illusion of Hitler discussing his personal experiences and plans to create his "new

Germany." In the beginning, Hitler chose "Four and a Half Years of Struggle against Lies, Stupidity, and Cowardice" to be the title for the book. The publisher, however, shortened his title down by changing it to Mein Kampf, which translates to My Struggle or My Battle.

In the novel, Hitler shows his depraved character through categorizing individuals based on their race as well as physical features. The book has established classes that included Aryans being deemed to be the best and pure. Hitler declares the Aryan as the perfect and superior of all human race. In line with Hitler's notion regarding Aryan supremacy, he claims the existence of another race that is inferior to the Aryans. In the middle of the list are the Jews, Roma, and the other non-Aryans. The excerpt in the book Hitler states:

"...it (Nazi philosophy) is not a firm believer in equality between races

However, in addition to the differences between them, it acknowledges the importance of their differences and is obligated to advocate for the victories over the more powerful and superior and demands the submission to the weaker and inferior according to the eternal Will of God that governs the world."

He goes on in different chapters to speak of Aryan superiority in comparison to other races.

"All the human culture, all the results of art, science, and technology that we see before us today, are almost exclusively the creative product of the Aryan... Hence, it is no accident that the first cultures arose in places where the Aryan, in his encounters with lower peoples, subjugated them and bent them to his will. They then became the first technical instrument in the service of a developing culture."

Hitler is still promoting his stance by asserting that people who dominate enjoy the advantages of being subjugated because they are near their superiors (the Aryans). Being close to them gives "weak" people an opportunity to gain knowledge from the dominant people (Aryan). Hitler is trying to stop his "pollution" of the Aryan race by threatening them with cautions. Hitler states that Aryans will be outstanding. He also urges Aryans to refrain from interfering and marriage with the "weaker" ethnic group. This is the only way to maintain the "master" status.

This book clears Hitler's anger towards Jews. Jewish community. Hitler claims that Jews are conspiring to prevent the Jews have a plan to stop the Aryans from taking over its proper place as the rulers in the world by altering its cultural and racial pure. The Jews claim to make up the structures of governments which require

Aryans to accept the equality of all races and are not conscious of the racial power they have.

"The mightiest counterpart to the Aryan is represented by the Jew."

The book also portrays Hitler's ideas about his struggle to rule the world in a continuous race, culture and political battle that pitted the Aryans against Jews. The philosophies of Hitler are described throughout the work. Hitler rails against the Jews as part of a worldwide conspiracy to take over the financial affairs of the world. Hitler states that Jews plan to dominate the media. He also accuses Jews of establishing a plethora of democratic systems, e.g., communalism.

According to Hitler that the Jews are the ones responsible to encourage prostitution, among other vices. The book also states that the Jews plan to make use of this ethos in order to create conflicts.

Hitler makes use of the text to promote hatred towards the Jews through referring to the Jews as Vermin and fibbers. They are also described as murky and cunning. clever, and smart, with no authentic cultural background parasite, broker, an insect that is young forever blood suckers, nauseating and dishonest brutes strangers, a threat, brutal hungry, the destructive threat to Aryan humanity and also the mortal foe of Aryan humanity, etc.

"...for the greater it gets greater, the more appealing the dream that was promised to him once rises through the haze of history and, with an euphoric enthusiasm the sharpest of minds can see the vision of dominance over the world is tangibly near."

The Nazis will take Hitler's conspiracy theories and the idea of "competition" for the domination of the globe in the world between Jews and Aryans in order to use the concept as a legitimate reason for the extermination of Jews. In conjunction with Hitler's assertion of ethnicity towards the Jews this doctrine would be spread throughout Germany and even into other territories occupied by Germany. The common doctrine drove towards the extermination of Jews who were active members of Nazism. Nazi party.

Alongside the calls to exterminate those who are Jews, Mein Kampf offers reasons for the attacks which Hitler as well as the greater Germany were later to launch. Hitler is of the opinion that the dominant race is entitled to vast areas of land as well as "living space," acquired via force or by natural means. It is his desire to consolidate even further Lebensraum (living area) by launching armed attacks on Poland, Belgium, the Soviet Union, and the Netherlands.

In order to achieve the status of a "superpower," Hitler declares, "Germany must first overthrow its old foe, France." The plan is viewed as a retribution mission to during the First World War, in which Hitler believed that the Germans were betrayed. Hitler willfully recounts of events that it is believed that Germany was prevented victory by internal troops.

In the 2nd volume of Mein Kampf, Hitler puts all the blame on Jews in the Mein Kampf, and warned "pure" Germans of the Jewish perfidy.

The first time the book was launched, the book had at best a poor rating in terms of sales. The book did not live up to the expectations of those who were expecting the stories from Hitler's unsuccessful coup.

In addition, the mastery of language was not great, presenting an uninformed man. But, after Hitler was appointed chief of the state of Germany at the time of 1933, novels were a huge success, selling millions of copies. In 1933, the Nazis thought it to be an integral element of their lives and their war on their adversaries. Mein Kampf was read at schools and considered a worthy present to people in Germany with a shared conviction. In light of the level of transparency the book offered, Hitler later showed regret creating the book. These revelations showed the personality of Hitler as well as his grand strategies to create his "new Germany" community, which he would, in the end, remain hidden.

Hitler's War Against the Jews

It is said that the Nazi head, Adolf Hitler, had terrible hatred for Jews and referred to them as a source of impurity to German superiority, as well as a scourge for his German community. However, his views were described by Holocaust survivors, Saul Friedlander, as "redemptive anti-Semitism." The author further states that Hitler set out to restore Germany from the social ills and illnesses that plagued its public and private spheres. But, Hitler opposed the Jewish principles that threatened the supremacy of Germans. They believed that the Jews believed in society's impartiality and the sympathy of the weak. They posed a challenge to Hitler's idea of restoring the natural order. The goal means the elimination of fragile (dependent) race. In the world of Hitler the dominant race possessed unlimited power against those of the "inferior" race. The idea was developed by Hitler that when the forces of such are resisted, the powerful get weakened, infested and begin to become impure.

What's known as a "war against the Jews" began with Hitler's desire to expand the boundaries of Germany in order to ensure food security and other supplies, which were scarce in Europe. After the First World War, the Allied forces had refused Germany colonies in Africa. The first decision Hitler made when the time he was elected in 1933 was to end any disapproval of the government and consolidate the power of his government. Reforming Germany started with a war in Jews. Jewish community. The Nazis placed an embargo over Jewish trade in April 1933. A few days later, the Jewish people in the civil service saw decreases, and by the end in May 1933, German schools were a closed zone for Jewish students. In the days that followed, Nazi students storming library and bookshops, attempting to remove any books which were in opposition to Nazi ideology, as well as those that were written by authors who weren't Aryans. In order to symbolically purify the German cultural heritage, students, along with their teachers, smuggled the books on the burning fire.

"Where one burns books, one will, in the end, burn people," wrote Heinrich Heine.

In the words of a German-Jewish poet The Nazis about eight years after the destruction of books to begin burning the Jews.

Extermination of the Jews

The eradication of Jews began with the need to German Law to distinguish the Aryans from Jews. This provision was designed to protect the honor, blood, as well as the rules and regulations for Reich citizens. The Law came to be a cornerstone of good judgment against Jews. The Law banned marriages that were intermarriages between German with Jewish descent as well as "Pure-blooded" Germans. It also provided Germans the right to political and civil rights, at the expense of those who were Jews.

Phase 1: Categorization

The categorizing of Germans as well as Jews is believed as the initial phase which brought about the destruction of Jews. In 1889, the Nurnberg Law officially categorized German as well as Jews. Although the Law didn't provide a definitive description as to German or Jew however, it did create an obstacle between these two races. The Law didn't consider Jews as religious groups or a weak race which did not merit the same treatment as others Germans. The law was passed in November of 1933. Law established two types of Jews that were: the first comprised Jews who had at least three grandparents. The second category comprised of the Jew people with two or less grandparents (also called "mongrels"). This description offered a disputed definition of what constitutes a "Jew", rooted not in the religion or identity however, but rather the bloodline.

Phase 2: The Resistance

As a response to the rising of Hitler In response to the rise of Hitler, Jews believed it was necessary to safeguard their status as Germans. Jew journalist Robert Weltsch, urged his colleagues Jews to "wear their identity with pride." In the context of the German soldiers who fought during the First World War, the Jews were horrified being deemed to be less Germans. This heightened the rage of Jews by final days of 1933. This led to an increase in Zionist militants. Others of the most prominent personalities voiced their displeasure and led their followers to fight the Nazis who oppressed the Jews. Martin

Buber, a devout Jewish philosopher, advocated for an increase in Jewish adult education as was described "preparations for the long journey ahead." Another Jew figure was the Rabbi Leo Baeck, spread prayer to mark the day of atonement. The prayer contained an appeal to resist. Leo Baeck stated, "We bow down before G-d; we stand erect before man." While only a few Jews could have predicted the result of the struggle, nobody could have imagined how risky the situation could be. The Jews did not appeal for assistance.

In 1939, at the close of the year by the end of 1939, a lot of Jews had reached the end of their line in finding refugee states. There were a few who managed to obtain visas for emigration towards in the United States of America and Palestine and Israel, opening the doors to Jew refugees. Others, however, did not want to take the entry of a lot of refugees. This proved to be to be a problem. To respond to the appeal of Jewish refugees in refugees from the United States of America and the other European countries met in France to discuss the matter. In the end, U.S. president, Franklin D. Roosevelt (did not attend) also invited the heads of state to be a part of the resettlement plan. He also noted that the states will not require the states to alter their laws, or dedicate money from government sources to the program and that they would only be able to use money from charitable sources for the resettlement plan. At the end of the day, states had less to do in on the subject of settling Jews.

In the wake of the failure of the plan to seek refuge in different nations, Jews were forced to be in the hands of Nazi radicals. In 1938 it was the year that the Nazis organized an anti-Jewish riot across in the Reich (including Austria). In just two weeks, the Nazis have set on fire the streets, stolen or destroyed synagogues as well as destroyed Jewish business. Over 250,000 Jewish individuals were detained and detained in prison camps. The discerning nature of Jews could be seen among the others in the community when the police sat by and watched the chaos without offering help as well as firefighters who fought the burning fire in order to keep it from spreading into adjacent Aryan business. Then, in the end it was decided that the Jews decided to accept the fate they were handed: They were not guaranteed an opportunity to live in Germany.

Phase 3: Oppressive Laws and Restrictions

In a somewhat contradictory way in a more contradictory sense, the Jewish community was required to settle a penalty of 1 billion Reichsmarks to compensate for the harm they caused to the German economy. Additionally they were also made to pay for the Jews had to pay up the damages caused by the unrest. Another restraining law was imposed as a threat to Jews. Jewish community. The law banned the taking of money from insurance companies by German Jews. An order of restraining was placed to stop the Jew populace from the most famous places of social gatherings. They were compelled to stay away from German schools, and to travel with their own private compartments in trains. These strict restrictions came to earlier prohibitions which made it impossible to Jews to pursue college degrees, run an enterprise, or practise law or medicine for people who weren't Jewish. As part of a plan known as the "Aryanization," the Nazis kept securing the property of Jews. The horrors suffered by Jews could be summarized in the Goring expression:

"I would not like to be a Jew in Germany!"

Victims of the Nazis' Brutality

Although Jews were Jews were at the heart of the Nazis"extermination plan," others were also subject to the brutalities. This group of people was targeted much further than Jews. People were targeted because they opposed the main beliefs of the Nazis and others were murdered for refusing part in Nazi programmes. Social equalityists as well as political rebels and trade unionists were among the first category of people who were taken into custody and detained in prison camps.

The Nazis were also responsible for the imprisonment of more than a quarter of a million Jehovah's Witness members due to their failure to declare allegiance to both the state as well as Hitler. Detainees were however offered the choice to renounce their religion to gain their freedom. A few chose to apostasy but the majority opted for martyrdom.

The Nazis also were also a target for Germans who were of African descendance (mostly often referred to as "Rhineland bastards"). They were the children of German mothers as well as French African troops who occupied the Rhineland following the First World War. The persecutions weren't as systematic. The Nazis effectively sterilized their victims. They believed that the Nazis believed that German from African origin could multiply in number and "pollute" the population, which would reduce their status as a "pure" German race. The Roma as well as Sinti (Gypsies) also were both targeted for exclusion. They were both targeted for gassing within concentration camps. Roma as well as Sinti were also referred to as "racial polluters." Their identification as social could be the rationale behind their plight and the massacre.

The Euthanasia Program

Following the start in the Second World War, the Germans initiated The T4 Program, also known as the "Euthanasia program". This plan aimed at "wiping out" all people who were disabled in Germany. The whole thing shook Hitler's idea of Aryan dominance. This group of Germans were referred to as "useless eaters" and "unworthy of life." The Nazis have cited the rationality of money as the primary reason for their exile. The gas chambers and crematoria was a standard methods of oppression used in the T4 Program.

The German crowd protested against the murders. A number of religious leaders, including Clemens August (Roman catholic bishop) opposed the plan and demanded it be stopped. Yet it was not enough, as the Nazis kept secretly pursuing those with disabilities.

The policies of German on occupation focused mainly on Jews as well as non-Jewish Poles in the aftermath of the invading of Poland. Hitler's quest for "village space" sought to stop the Polish national identity and community. The Nazis destroyed Polish politicians and religious leaders. They smashed the Polish administration and seized the children of a select group of Polish. Children were raised to be "voluntary Aryans" by their newly-adopted German "parents." Many Poles were forced to the gruelling and solitary work of food regimens for survival. A few were stripped of their property and evicted to be incarcerated in camps of concentration.

The Expansion of German and Formation of Ghettoes

In contrast against contrary to the German policy of eradicating Jews and eliminating the Jewish community within Germany In contrast to the German policy of extermination, territorial expansion brought in more Jews under the supervision of Germany. The annexed areas of Austria as well as Sudetenland (currently located in now in Czech Republic) brought more Jews under the control of Germany. The war led to additional attacks. In the aftermath, the "Jewish question" became an important issue, after the invading of Poland. Two million Jews were under the rule of Germany in the aftermath of the division of Poland into Germany as well as Germany and the Soviet Union. In the years following, as the desire to rid the Jews increased as the war raged on, the Nazis considered exile the Jewish people to the island of Madagascar. Due to the lack of resources to carry out the deportation process and the lack of resources, the Nazis dismissed the idea because it was unreal. In addition, the conflict on the ocean posed a danger to Germany that had never won during the Battle of Britain. The decision to enter the sea would mean entering into a conflict which they already ended.

The expanding Jewish populace led to the formation of the Jewish council headed by Reinhardt Heydrich in 1939. The council was made up of 24 rabbis, as well as Jewish leadership. It was accountable to the German management and enacted the execution of German directives. After the creation of the Warsaw Ghetto (the largest ghetto in Poland) and the Jewish residents were confined to less than 3 percent of the region, yet it was the largest segment of the Warsaw inhabitants. A flurry of diseases as well as malnutrition, hunger and affected this community long before the initial Germany bullet was fired.

Ghettoes' establishment was seen as a temporary step by the German administration. Ghettoes were intended to hold Jews Jews until a permanent solution for their population discovered. In contrast they Jews were of the opinion they'd be kept within the ghettos till the conclusion of the Second World War. The Jews believed that they could make Ghetto living a lot more durable, even in extreme circumstances. The Jews discovered alternatives to the restricted rights. They turned to underground schools, after they were told that the Nazis banned them from school. They kept their faith in secret and lived a faith-based lives. They mainly used music and humor in defiance. As time went on, and the inhumane treatment continued, Jews were forced to resort to violent protests.

Mass Killings

There was a precise time frame for when the first steps were taken to begin the systematic extermination of Jews. It is believed that the "final solution to the Jewish question" remains a vague strategy which no one is able to determine what it was or when it began (whether it was an unilateral decision or the result of a sequence of carefully crafted decisions). However they did, and the Nazis started the systematic elimination of the Jewish people in the month of June 1941, with an strike on the Soviet Union, a once-aligned all-time ally of Germany.

Germany used a mobile killer unit within the territory in the Soviet Union. The soldiers were instructed to shoot Jews, Soviet commissars, as well as Roma within the regions that were conquered. They were, sometimes, assisted by local police forces and communities of native anti-

Semitism, and the Axis troopers in seizing the victims before taking them away to be killed. The Einsatzgruppe known as the killing troop has killed over 33,000 Jews in Kyiv as well as the Babi Yar. Further Jews (approximately 28 thousand) were executed within Rumbula Forest, outside the town of Riga, Latvia. Seventy thousand additional Jews were murdered during the battle of Vilna (currently Vilnius). Then, at the Ninth Fort, the troops executed a total of nine thousand Jews as well as children. The attacks on the Jews continued to be a constant threat until that the Soviet Union struck a retaliation strategy. At the end of the day, the killer units returned to pick up the dead bodies of those killed by Jews and then burn them to make evidence of the murder. The offensive was believed to have claimed around 150,000 of people, mainly Jews. But, locals were enraged at their Jewish neighbors and let German troops be the ones to responsibility for the deaths. Being surrounded by German soldiers could, during the time, trigger unrest and even massacre. In the Baltics Nationalist groups were enraged at the Jews as well, and killed the Jews in large huge numbers.

Jewish Resistance

Furthermore, the allies were prepared to strike at the smallest incident and they were completely determined to ensure that an "final solution" come to realization. Additionally being adamant, the Nazis were willing to go to great lengths to hide their actions in order in order to deflect international scrutiny. The German strategy of reciprocal retaliation meant that it was difficult for Jews living in ghettos to stand up to.

The situation was altered after Germany eventually ordered the closing of the ghettoes. This made the Jew community conscious of the death they were facing. The Jew group decided to hold an array of protests in the ghettoes, forests, as well as the concentration camps. The Jews were fighting on their own, but often, in conjunction with the various resistance groups from Russia, France, and Yugoslavia. The Jews launched a single-to-one revolt after they saw their imminent loss of life.

In April 1943, a junior Jew, Mordecai Anielewicz, took over the Warsaw Ghetto Uprising following the an mass expulsion of Jews to Treblinka, a concentration camp at Treblinka. Aside from Vilna Realizing the intent of German policies towards those who were Jew, Abba Kovner mounted in armed struggle from November 1941. Kovner took the lead in combat against the Germans all through September 1943. Then, in March of 1943 gay community, their sympathizers and activists under the leadership of Willem Arondeus bombed the registry in Amsterdam in order to erase the lists of Jews and others who were who were hunted by Nazis. As with the Warsaw Ghetto revolt, Treblinka and Sobibor have also fought for their rights in terror of being killed at the camps of extermination. As the massacre was about to conclusion in 1944 in 1944, the "special commando" unit in Auschwitz killed a funeral home.

As the advance of allies in 1944 The Nazis most of them, those in the security service at the death camps, desperate sought to clear the camps and hide their activities. To avoid leaving any evidence The security forces took prisoners westward and forced them to move into the middle of German territories. More than 50 "death marches" from the concentration camps for the extermination of prisoners as Nazi dominance slowly dwindled to its ending.

Inmates were given a meager or no water and food as well as were not permitted to stop for rest during the journey. Anyone who was unable to keep up or were unable to continue the marches were killed instantly.

A few days before the appearance of the red army at Auschwitz The Nazis drove more than 60 thousands of people from Wodzislaw and then put the people on freight trains (mostly open vehicles) towards the Holocaust concentration camps of Gross-Rosen, Dachau, Mauthausen and Buchenwald. The statistics show that one out of four died on their way to Auschwitz. In the months of April and May 1945 American as well as British forces traveling to military objectives, walked into the death camps of the west. They were witness to what transpired. While tens of thousands of prisoners had died but the camps were not the most deadly. Even for soldiers who claimed that they'd grasped the most horrific sight and whiffs and the dead bodies the encountered have left a lasting impression.

Conditions of prisoners were so bad that many ended up dying after their release. In Dachau in Germany, soldiers encountered railway vehicles that were able to explode with bodies. In certain camps, soldiers set them on fire in order to stop the spreading of the typhus. The survivors' liberation was never a time of victory. Viktor Frankl, a survivor of Auschwitz is a recollection of:

"Everything was a lie. It was as if it were a dream. The only time, for some it was much earlier or not at all -- was liberation truly being liberating."

The governments of the allied countries who previously received information regarding the calamity did not launch an attempt to help the Jews. Allies didn't bomb the railroad tracks that lead to concentration camps. To the allies, the current war was extremely important, and only once they had won, was they able to participate in the rescue of Jews. The actions were not taken upon explicitly in order to end the mass murder. A memo by an U.S. general counsel to the U.S. Secretary of the Treasury, Henry Morgenthau, declared the policy that was implemented by the U.S. state department an "acquiescence to the murder of the European Jews." In response to the criticism, condemnation as well as the memo Morgenthau helped to establish the War Refugee Board, making a late, ineffective attempt to save dying Jews mostly through the international community and strategy.

Chapter 8: Events Leading to the Attack

Historical Anti-Semitism and the Rise of Adolf Hitler

Prior to the Holocaust it was evident of hostility towards the Jews. One example of this is the desecration of Jewish synagogues as well as the forceful expulsion from Palestine in the hands of Romans. At that time, although there was a huge backing for the Jewish populace and the elite of education argued the acceptance of religion.

Furthermore, the time of Napoleon witnessed a shift in laws that brought an end to Jewish restriction. The other European politicians also followed the same path between the late 17th as well as 18th century. However, despite all this effort however, anti-Semitism continue to be a problem throughout Europe. It was a matter of route of race, rather than the spiritual path. This is evidence of hate towards Jews and the Jew community didn't begin in the era of Hitler. Yet, Hitler remains a compelling figure in the propagation of the idea of.

The literature and the history of our times don't provide the first source of the most vile kind of anti-Semitism embraced by Hitler as well as the Nazis. A superficial knowledge has, at times, taken from the time of Hitler's being prisoner. Hitler was born in Austria around 1889. He was an officer in the German troops that were involved during the First World War. Hitler along with the majority of Germans was adamant about the Jewish people for the demise of Germany during the conflict. After the conclusion of the First World War, Hitler was a part of with the German Workers' Party and then changed its name to the known Nazis. Involvement with the Beer Hall Putsch in 1923 led to him being imprisoned on treason-related charges. In prison the author wrote his memoir called Mein Kampf. In the book, Hitler forecasted the annihilation of the Jewish race in Germany.

Hitler's hatred of his fellow Jews was motivated by his abstinence from the notion of "pure German superiority" and the desire to make enough room for Nazis. In the decade following his release, Hitler banked on the weak points of his adversaries in order to boost the standing for the Nazis and eventually ascend to authority. Hitler was named chancellor of Germany in the beginning of January 1933 in addition to appointing himself the ultimate leader of Germany after the demise of the president Paul Von Hindenburg in 1934.

The Nazi Revolution

In the midst of the Hitler regime was his ideas about German race purity as well as the expansion plan. These ideas were adopted into the 1933 year the year he was elected to power and set out to establish both domestic and foreign policy. At first his first days, the Nazi supremacist would only issue brutal prosecutions of Communists and leaders of the opposition. In 1933, the call to eliminate any opposition German led to the creation of Dachau's first prison at Dachau in the month of March, 1933. It was the prison of communists and generals of the opposition.

Dachau turned into a gruesome scene under the supervision under the supervision of Heinrich Himmler. The year was July the other camps were already being constructed for communists, rebels as well as foreigners. Then in the year, the Nazis developed their "Aryanization" strategy, aimed to eliminate foreigners, mainly Jews out of the civil service, eliminating Jewish firms, and depriving Jewish doctors and lawyers of clients. In 1939, the Nuremberg Law was established to define Jews as well as half-breeds.

The Law was a tool of Jew discrimination, resentment, and ill-treatment. This bloody saga culminated on"the night of broken glass, "night of broken glass" during which Jewish business were burnt window smashed, Jewish businesses burned, and synagogues razed. That day, thousands of Jews were shot dead, and hundreds were detained.

The Beginning of the War

The war's beginning was followed with the German invasion of Poland in 1939. Then, in the years to come, German troops forced thousands of Polish Jews from their homes and forced them into Ghettos. Their possessions confiscated by the Jews were handed over to Germans (those living in other countries) Germany) as well as polish gentiles. The walls were high around the ghettos for confinement and served as prisons for cities-states. They were also used as prisons for city-states. Jewish Councils governed the ghettos. Because of the ghetto's congestion and lack of sanitation, the Ghettos quickly become an ideal breeding ground for diseases, e.g., typhus.

In the 1930s, the Nazis established the "Euthanasia" program in which gassing was used to death of nearly 70 thousand Germans who were diagnosed with brain disorders. Hitler had to stop the program in 1941 due to the protests of German religious authorities. Yet, his forces continue to murder disabled people behind closed doors. Death tolls reached an around two hundred and seventy-five thousand before 1945. What is believed of the day was that Euthanasia program was the catalyst for the start of the Holocaust.

The Beginning of the "Final Solution"

The German troops conducted success in expansion efforts throughout Europe during the period 1940 under the direction of Hitler. They defeated Denmark, Norway, Netherlands, Belgium, France, and Luxembourg. As the war was in progress, Jews from all over Europe and European Gypsies were displaced and detained to Polish ghettos. The first step towards a ultimate solution occurred on June 11, 1941, the time that Germany began to invade the Soviet Union, killing more than half a million during the war. The German forces used mobile troops to strike, shooting at people who had been Soviet Jews.

The 31st of July, 1941, Hitler's most powerful commanding officer, Hermann

Goering, drafted memos to the top official of the security department that emphasized the need to find a solution in the case of "the Jewish question." The next step was the labeling of the entire population of Jews with the yellow star, which exposed Jews to dangers that awaited them. These ensuing controversies culminated with the exile of Jews to Polish Ghettoes as well as others cities controlled by German during the USSR.

The first week of June 1941 witnessed the first experimental executions at the concentration camps, including Auschwitz. German doctors tested the efficacy of certain treatments, employing Jews as the guinea pigs. In August of that year, German officials employed Zyklon-B as a pesticide that gassed over 500 Soviet Jews to death. Security officials at the time commanded the pesticide to be used in large quantities, a warning of the Holocaust in the future.

Holocaust Death Camps

The start of Holocaust concentration camps were marked with the transport of Jews from the ghettoes into specific concentration camps. The removal from the Ghettos was conducted with a well-organized method. The military identified the majority of those thought of as infirm, sick, or old for the first round of transport. Between 1942 and 1945 in 1942-1945, the Jewish community was threatened with deportation with great force to prison camps all across the continent, which included the entire states that were allies to Germany. This deportation plan resulted in the rise of the Warsaw Ghetto Uprising in 1943. Warsaw Ghetto inhabitants rose to their arms to protest against the regime, which caused hunger and disease to those living there. This revolt culminated in the deaths of more than 7000 Jews. Over 50 thousand Jews who were able to survive the aftermath of the rebellion were placed in concentration camps. It was the Warsaw Ghetto revolt inspired mass protests across a variety of camps and Ghettos throughout Germany and across Europe.

In the beginning, Nazis kept the massacre as a secret. But the sheer number of victims was difficult to cover up for a lengthy duration. Eyewitnesses and survivors who escaped from prisons took on the story of the mass murders in Europe and attracted the attention of Allied Forces. The Allied government would then receive a lot of criticism over failing to act or even make news of the massacres at the camps known to the public. It was clear that the Allied forces were at the time, focussed on winning the battle. The government has since provided their reasons for not taking action. The Allied Governments expressed a general skepticism regarding the Holocaust reports, as well as the fear and repudiation of the possibility that carnage like this could happen as well, in an such large amount.

The most famous and most infamous extermination camp Auschwitz was constructed using the form of three structures. It was a jail camp (Auschwitz I) as well as an extermination camp (Auschwitz II-Birkenau) and the slave labor camp (Auschwitz III-Buna-Monowitz). When they arrived at Auschwitz there, Auschwitz Jews were subjected to a selection procedure. An German physician was the one who supervised the process of selection. The purpose of the process was to distinguish pregnant women, sick older people, as well as those who were well-built and healthy Jews. The fit Jews were forced into work, while those who were not were destined for immediate execution.

The companies that were located near Auschwitz like IG Farben, enjoyed the huge workforce available and put a huge amount of capital into the production process. The company believed that working for a wage would become a long-lasting part of economic activity. The Jewish had to be beaten until death with no shelter, food, clothing and medical care. At times, Germans were able to conduct another screening exercise, then move the prisoners who were able to perform the work into the gas chambers in Birkenau. Contrary to the camps at Auschwitz and Majdanek where prisoners were used for support in the Germany participation in wartime and the camps of Belzec, Treblinka, and Sobibor were purely killing areas.

The most shocking massacre in camp was held in Auschwitz. Around 2 million prisoners died in Auschwitz by themselves in a manner similar to an enormous industrialized system. Auschwitz was a place of death for millions. Auschwitz contained the Jews and prisoners of non-Jewish origin. The only difference was that the Jew group was gassed in the course of treatment. Many others also fell victim to hunger and diseases. The year 1943 was when the eugenicist Josef Mengele visited the Auschwitz for a series of research studies. The doctor, who was also known as"the "Angel of Death", conducted experiments on Jewish prisoners, most of them twins, using injections.

The causes of the Holocaust by time:

30 January 1933: Hitler's election as chancellor for Germany

At this time, the President Hindenburg was invited by President Hindenburg Hitler to retake the post of Chancellor of Germany in the wake of a protracted vote.

February 27 33 February 27, 1933: The Reichstag fire

Berlin's parliament has been set on fire. It is the Nazi administration declares a state-of-emergency after the incident that caused the fire and then arrests and executes Dutch radical named Marinus Van der Lubbe.

March 5, 1933: The Reichstag Elections

After the burning of the Parliament following the burning of the parliament, a vote for the legislature was carried out in March of 1933. The Nazis received 44% of votes. This was not democratic because many of the opposition's leaders were already exiled.

March 22nd, 1933: the founding of Dachau

A concertation camp is erected in Dachau close to Munich for the purpose of housing the political prisoners who are predominantly communists. Later that day is the day that it is passed the Enabling Act is passed, giving the state authority to rule for four years.

April 1, 1933: The Boycott

This day marks the date that the Nazi government calls for a national boycott on all Jewish-owned companies. This is the first major action taken against Jews.

April 7th the 7th of April, 1933: The Reforms in the public service.

The Nazi regime adopts a law that reforms the service of public employees. Jews are exempt from civil service. The president Hindenburg allows the Jew frontline soldiers from that First World War from the prohibition.

10 May 1933: Fire of books

Nazi students as well as their instructors take over bookstores and libraries. They take away all books that were written by Jews or other non-Aryans and then set them on fire in public.

* July 11, 1933: Sterilization Law

The Nazi government adopts a law that prevents those with disabilities as well as other diseases that are hereditary to spread. The law was put into place in 1934, resulting in more than 4000 individuals sterilized.

* September 22: The law on the Reich Chamber of Culture

The bill passes, prohibiting Jews as well as other non-Aryans from taking part in German cultural practices. The law bans

Jews from attending theatres or other events held in public.

* August 2nd, 1934: Death of Hindenburg

German President Paul von Hindenburg dies. After his death, Hitler anoints himself as the Reichsfuehrer, the highest head of Germany.

* September 15, 1935: Anti-Semitic Law

Hitler proclaims that the Anti-Semitic Nuremberg Laws at a Nazi gathering. Nuremberg Laws Nuremberg Laws are made up of two distinct rules, the first being the Law on the Protection of German Blood and German Honor as well as the 'Reich Citizenship Law.

*July 12, 1936: Another camp for concentration

The second concentration camp was constructed in Oranienburg near Berlin and serves as an incarceration facility. The third camp will be constructed on the 15th of July 1937 at Buchenwald.

12 March 1938: The annexed territory of Austria

This date marks the day that German troops invading and annexing Austria. Over two hundred thousand Jews within Austria are subject to similar anti-Semitic laws to German Jews.

* 14 June 1938: Registration is compulsory for Jewish firms

The Nazi government has declared that any business that are owned by Jews need to be registered and designated as Jewish. The following day sees the deportation of "asocial" Jews. Every Jew who has a previous conviction is detained and taken to the execution camps in Buchenwald, Dachau, and Sachsenhausen.

* 9 November 1938 The pogrom

In the night of the 9th and 10th of November the Nazis take over Jewish firms, smashing windows, and pillaging. Synagogues are destroyed and stained. There are many Jews get killed and some are detained and put in camps for concentration. In the next five days and all Jewish students are removed out of German schools.

* September 1, 1938: Operation T4

This date marks the day that Hitler allows the operation "Euthanasia". Disabled people are rounded up and murdered, which includes children. The program ceases however, it continues secretly until 1945 when the conflict ends.

* 23rd November 1939 All Jews living in Poland are required to wear an armband that displays the green Star of David in public.

* 16 October 1940: The inauguration of the Warsaw Ghetto

The Warsaw Ghetto, the largest of all Jewish Ghettos, was founded in 1940. The Ghetto was then closed on the 15th of November 1940.

* March 1, 1941: Construction of Auschwitz-Birkenau

The construction of the second section of Auschwitz (Birkenau) was established on March 1st, 1941. This area would eventually become the most brutal and crowded section in the prison. The majority of the gassing and burning of Jews occurred in the wing that was part of Auschwitz. On the 22nd of September, 1941 the first experiment in gassing occurred at Auschwitz. The camp for concentration of Belzec would be later founded in November 1st of the same year.

* July 15 to October 28: Deportations

In the time between, Jews were deported from Amsterdam and the Warsaw Ghetto and Theresienstadt and to various camps of extermination, including Auschwitz as well as the Treblinka.

* 19 April 1943 * April 19, 1943 Warsaw Ghetto uprising

After mass deportation into extermination camps, as well as the end of the process of eliminating the Warsaw Ghetto, Jews held a armed protest on the streets. The Germans started torching the ghetto in the days which followed, shooting every Jew trying to flee away from burning homes. The Warsaw rebellion would eventually lead to a an uprising similar to that at Treblinka on the 2nd August 1943.

* On the 17th of January 1945 on the 17th of January 1945, the Soviet Union army would come to rescue and free the

remaining 75,000 five hundred prisoners of Auschwitz.

Part II: Living to Tell the Story--Survivor Stories

Once we have a better understanding about what Holocaust was about, we can now dive into the memories of a few survivors. It might give us some more insight into the atrocities that were perpetrated against them in the detention center at Auschwitz prison camp. Should we? We will discuss it in the chapters to follow.

Chapter 9: The Story of Irene Fogel Weiss

Irene Fogel Weiss was born on the 21st of November 30th, 1930 on the 21st of November, 1930 in Botragy, Czechoslovakia, currently called Batrad, Ukraine. Parents included Leah Fogel and Meyer. When she was younger her mother worked as employed as a domestic worker, and her dad, Meyer was the owner of a lumberyard for his family. The money from sales helped her parents to support them. Five siblings were hers, which included: Reuven, Moshe, Serena, Edit, and Gershon.

Botragy was a small township situated in Czechoslavakia which had an estimated 1,000 people which included around the ten Jewish families. Her early life was marked by the poverty of the people around her. The majority of her neighbours practiced agriculture as their sole source of income. Apart from that, small-time cash-making activities like selling vegetables as well as tailoring and shoe making dominated the township. Because of their connection and commonality, residents who lived in the township had a good relationship.

Following the Holocaust She emigrated into New York in 1947, and was wed with Martin Weiss in 1949. By 1953, the couple had moved into Northern Virginia. Then, she enrolled in the Bachelor of Arts Degree in Education from one of the American University, which enabled her to work at the Fairfax school for children in the public sector, Virginia 13 years. Presently, she together with Martin, her partner Martin have three kids and four grandchildren. She volunteers at the U.S. Holocaust Memorial Museum. However the elder sister of her currently lives within New Jersey.

Her Ordeal

Trouble began in the tuft she was living in (Botragy) about 1938. The girl was just eight when she was in that time. The township she lived in was added to Hungary following the time her nation had fallen in two. Hungary is a German-owned country, embraced anti-Semitic beliefs against the Jew inhabitants of their newly acquired territory. Therefore, all Jews and her entire family, were subject to humiliation and sexism from the invading Nazis. The law was not in place protecting them as well as their belongings. This meant that the majority of the property was squandered and handed over to non-Jews. As an example, her father's lumber business was taken by his hands and handed over to the non-Jew.

Additionally, they faced discrimination throughout the world they could not make use of public facilities like trains, schools, or the public parks, because of the hatred and violence towards the minority group. In the end, they hid behind others of their race, in order not to draw the attention of others. The wearing of an orange star was required for them to ensure they would be easily recognized and thus vulnerable to constant beatings by different races.

In addition, a large number of people who were of Jewish from various countries were forced to join work groups. They operated under the control of the army during 1942. The father of Irene was among the group, and after the period of six months, he returned to his home only to discover the Jew group being shackled to extreme living conditions.

The year 1944 was the time when the Hungarian government still had not given its Jewish populace in Auschwitz. Auschwitz prison camp. This meant that the Nazis were forced to enter Hungary and announce orders to the Hungarian government to gather all of the Jew inhabitants and then deport their bodies to the camps. This were the final words for the Jewish inhabitants of Hungary that included Irene's entire family. In April 1944, they were picked in a manner of animals, and then transferred to Munkacs ghetto. This was the main point of transit on cattle transport vehicles.

But, the place was not meant to accommodate people. it was an industrial brick factory. This meant that thousands of individuals lived in squalid in squalid conditions. There was an overcrowding problem with no bathroom facilities, and the one restroom that they could use was the trench constructed outside of the plant. When they arrived, women that were younger than 16 year old were promptly cut off; Irene was one of those. Her mother, however, gave her a scarf to cover her head that was bald and would help her survive the screening phase of Auschwitz. Auschwitz Concentration Camp. The headscarf would make her appear older than she actually was.

From the Munkacs ghettos They were then transported from Munkacs ghetto to Auschwitz by the same carts that they were brought with. In a span of just two months, more than 425 thousand Jews were exiled out of Hungary and brought to Auschwitz.

Most hurting her was the sudden and inhumane nature of the process of deportation was. Individuals who were close and had known each other for years were rudely and suddenly separated, without adequate notification. Additionally, they were allowed to go with one suitcase intended to be able to accommodate all their belongings from the past; this was extremely difficult. Her memory is vivid of the time her mother fought with the idea of putting their possessions in bags. There were too many items enough to make her unpack and pack numerous times. She was frustrated and decided to leave everything else behind in the room and packed only her bedding as well as food items, along with a warm blankets. After that, it was filled. In order to make it more manageable for her, she brought the wedding ring, the watch and a few earrings they could be able to exchange to buy food, if an opportunity came up. Following the day, the couple was taken to town hall, at which point her father was directed to give all his wealth to a gang comprised of the school's principal as well as the town's mayor.

Auschwitz was a baffling experience during the brief time she was in Earth It was totally different from the life she was accustomed to. Because of her age and her age, she was utterly shocked and terrified of the sights she witnessed, and was unsure of the reason they were sent there and what kind of mistakes they'd made that warranted the treatment they received. In the beginning, her father assumed that it was a camp for workers, because of the barracks, uniforms, and prisoners he saw as well as being optimistic, as he had heard reports of Jews being killed in Poland. So, being an inmate was an option that was pleasantly welcoming.

They initially thought at first that this was the result of discrimination. The people didn't know the extent to which they could be impacted. The Germans were planning a meticulous genocide scheme which they didn't know about. Therefore, they did not think of the mass murder of Jewish children in order to stop its growth.

Without any other choice to them at the moment, the majority were able to accept fate, but, they also had desire of seeing one another in the future. Unfortunately, this was not likely to happen. In their defense they Germans used deceitful tactics to entice their victims. In one instance, they let people Jewish believe that they were being enlisted to work as laborers, however actually, they were being killed via work. They also took them to the bathroom, but actually, they're going into a slaughterhouse among other aspects.

After their arrival Her family was split. The father and older brother were moved on one side, while her younger siblings and mom to the opposite side while her sister was on the other side. The girl couldn't resist holding onto her younger sister at first. In the end, she was escorted towards her mother's side and then she went towards the opposite side, which was where her sister's elder brother was. She had the chance to live.

They were unaware that they were subject to being photographed that was a directive from the top. Photos from Hungarian Jews arriving at the platform, as well as their experiences being dressed for prison and heading towards the baths were captured.

These photos helped her identify herself on the platform that she was waiting to arrive at following her separation from her sibling. In another photograph she could recognize her family as they head to the gas tank. A few of the family members on the picture comprised her mother and two brothers. The photo of her arriving was released a few years later in a publication called The Auschwitz Album by Yad Vashem. It was given in by her child. She believes that everything on the image depicts the events that transpired during her stay at the camp of concentration.

The father of the family was chosen to perform labor in the sonderkommando. This involved the taking dead bodies out of the slaughterhouses (gas chambers) as well as setting the fire to them. It was the norm for SS staff at the camp to kill sonderkommandos at the end of a certain time and take them over by new recruits. Later, she learned through her aunt that her father was murdered for refusing to carry out his duties as sonderkommando.

The psychological traumas designed to humiliate them upon their stay at treatment centers. The women there were stripped naked and shaving off their hair, including their pubic areas, by Jewish males. From the perspective of Irene, Nazis intended to humiliate and even kill Jews with no moral justification during the process. As she fumbled around trying to find her sister, she recalled being brought in the first line to the bathroom, and directed to search for her sister in the crowd of shaving faces. The entire group looked alike to her each when a door was unlocked.

After having a conversation, meeting and asking questions regarding the location of her brothers as well as her parents to a number of people who been there before They simply pointed out the chimneys. In the beginning, she didn't take the statements seriously, however it didn't take long to grasp and comprehend the events that were taking place. The crematorium's location provided her with a view that allowed her to observe hundreds of innocent children females, men and women waiting to enter the gas chambers, without having any idea the outcome to the people who were waiting there. A majority of them were killed in less than a half hour upon their arrival. the bodies of their victims were buried.

When they arrived the crematorium was in operation 24/7, devouring thousands of Hungarian Jews. The girl was fortunate to have been enlisted as a slave, along with her older sister Serena who was placed in the Birkenau area of the camp. They remained together for a large portion of their time, despite threats to split them.

A more comforting aspect of the chaos there was that they had the chance to get together with their older aunts. The aunts had two aunts, Piri and Rose both, barely in their 20s. This caused her to stop crying in just a few minutes. Being in an emotional situation stimulated and lifted them up, as well as provided them with the determination to make it through.

Four of them worked at an establishment that was known as"the "Canada" section, which was the name used to describe the store located near the funeral home IV. It was a place to store prisoners' clothing and other items. The prisoner's residence remained for 8 months, which ended in the beginning of January in 1985. In order to survive that time frame of 8 months, she needed to break free from her present. The horror and suffering was just too overwhelming to handle.

Most of the time she was able to pretend that she was in a fantasy but that what happened wasn't real and it would all come to an end and she would be able to survive. The way she lived was denial. She recounts how they visited the crematorium on a daily basis and witnessed how sonderkommandos ripped gold off the bones of dead people and couldn't keep the bodies in check which were growing each day. Also, they heard the constant crying in the gas chambers, and the constant burning of the fireplace, but opted to ignore it and did not wish to believe there was anything happening in the confines of their own. At other times she put her ear in a sock to stop the screaming while telling herself she'd one day return to her home. What was going on wasn't happening in the universe that she was aware of and was not her true self who was being affected by what was going on.

But, as Russian forces continued to advance in the direction of Germany, the Nazis began to realize they were on the bottom of the barrel; as a result they increased their efforts to eliminate the Jews. In this situation, it became a challenge for her to be aware of what was occurring in the surrounding area. The time was that the crematorium could not meet the killing pace. This forced the Nazis to burn corpses out in the open. Additionally, the amount of objects left in the location where she worked was increasing with alarming rapidity.

Due to the Soviet red army's advance in the month of January 1945, SS employees responsible for the camp began a compulsory match of the prisoners of the camp which led to many deaths. They were ordered to compete with Ravensbruck concentration camp, which was in Germany.

One of the reasons for most deaths was that prisoners were not wearing appropriate clothing suitable for the chilly winter conditions that prevailed during that time. Additionally, the majority suffered from ailments like dysentery and the typhoid virus, and hunger. In the course of the march, anyone who were tired and lagging were sprayed with bullets by SS staff. Anyone who stopped to tie shoelaces, or to urinate were targeted.

In the course of their transport in Neustadt-Glewe her aunt Piri became sick in the process of her death. Also, on a daily roll call, she was found to be with her older sister as well as a couple of slaves were separated from others, since they were thought to be thin and weak for all tasks.

But Irene explained to a guard Serena was her sibling, therefore she was required to be with her. She was then allowed to.

Others inmates together began to talk about the possibility of being returned into the main camp to be treated to gas because of their low status. Irene as well as her sister were confined to one room with others inmates to ensure that they would be able to wait until transportation back to camp. However, this never happened.

The increasing Soviet Union forces had caused the SS forces to leave to the outskirts of Moscow, leaving behind slaves and their camp that they left behind. This allowed prisoners to go home at any time. Irene and her aunt Rose as well as her older sister sought refuge in a secluded building located in the town nearby. They were responsible for themselves, especially since the Russians came in quick and then left without a reason.

The ladies took a little hours trying to get to Prague and discover their family. They found one of their uncles with an initials of Joseph Mermelstein. The man had left the town he grew up in and moved for Palestine in 1938 returning to fight in the military. Only a handful of aunts and uncles were able to survive the rough times. In the end, she as well as her sister Serena are the only child who made it through the entire family.

From Prague the group headed for Teplice-Sanov Sudetenland. When they began their stay in the new home they were unsure of how the events had affected others in the family as they did not access any electronic communication device, like phones. The names of those who survived were entered on lists and were pinned to the walls of most structures in the vicinity.

Meetups for refugees were filled with concerns about where to locate relatives and other family members. As a result she discovered that, out of one hundred residents deported from the town 10 people survived the experience. Two of them were children.

Every other child and parents were also killed in the camp of concentration. When they reached Sudetenland the aunt of her mother became in bed because of tuberculosis. The elder sister of her got an employment in a firm as she was enrolled in an institution in Czech. Through financial assistance from organizations like the Hebrew Immigrant Aid Society, as well as the support of relatives they were able to relocate from Prague to New York in the year 1947.

Chapter 10: The Story of David Mermelstein

David Mermelstein, currently eighty-six years old was born in Kivjazd, Czechoslovakia, in 1928. When he was fifteen years old, he was an Holocaust victim. As with all Jews who resided in Hungary following the breakup of Czechoslovakia He was taken into a shackle and sent to Auschwitz-Birkenau. The man was among the very last one-half million Jews to be taken in the camp. Following the experience the man was able get to America. He was 18 years old at the time. the age at that time, and settled in Brooklyn, New York, and then moved into Rhode Island.

Mermelstein became engaged to his bride in 1948. They later wed in the year 1949.

The couple honeymooned in Miami Beach, and it is their place of residence since. There are three kids with three grandchildren and one great-grandchild. Additionally, he is a part of the Holocaust survivors' foundation situated within the U.S. He aims to make sure that people in the world do not forget the horrors that occurred in the Holocaust in order that it will never occur again.

His Ordeal

David stated that he and others of the Jews were unaware of the meaning behind "Auschwitz" when they were being rounded up. Their only thought in their minds was that they had been transported to the camp. After being transferred around locations, including the Munkacs ghettos, they reached Auschwitz. Auschwitz prison camp.

At the time of arrival the group was arranged in five rows. Through a fence there were old women and people with walking sticks, people wearing stripes, playing Jewish songs, as well as young kids playing with ball as well as dolls, in addition to the many different activities happening.

Along with another hundred prisoners, they had an unassuming wagon that belonged to the notorious doctor. Josef Mengele, a person who was famous for the cruel and cruel treatment he administered to those in the camp.

The man greeted them and began the selection procedure. Wearing white gloves in his hands the his hands were covered in white gloves. Josef Mengele was known to glance at the prisoner and then move a small stick left or right in the process known as the selection procedure. In just a few seconds, prisoners fates were decided by the selection process: those who were going to be gassed as well as those who were going to work until the point of death. At this point nobody knew what would happen to them in the next. They were the ones who had been chosen to be executed were sent to the left side, and were required to walk for a distance about a half mile prior to getting to the gas chambers, and their the final location. Parents, younger siblings as well as grandparents were sent to the left side of the line, meaning that they would be dead within minutes of arriving at the gas stations.

When he stepped on his older brother's shoe, he was wrongly believed to be seventeen years older. So, he was told to turn to the right side, thereby to avoid the fate of relatives. As a result, along with his brother who was also booked, he had to be employed at the camp.

The people on the right that included him as well as his brother, were taken to a room inside the barracks. There, they were was instructed to remove their clothing. They were then provided with fresh outfits, which consisted of a shirt or cap as well as pants. Also, they were advised to keep their shoes for only a few hours.

When they inquired about the whereabouts of relatives, the guard led them to the front door and pointed out the fires, chimneys, and fumes emanating from the crematorium. He also informed them that they didn't have families.

In the camp, efforts from the previous guests to talk to the latest guests were ineffective because of the electric fence which separated the new arrivals from. Any person who tried to transmit messages across was destroyed. This was the moment that Mermelstein began to comprehend what the significance of the odor that spewed out of the chimneys.

He was also able to witness how some of the prisoners were electrocuted by hanging onto the fence. They realized there was no reason to live, and so they opted to die rather and work until they die. But his older brother who was in the same prison discouraged him from doing so since it was aiding the Nazis to achieve their goals.